# Knowing and Writing School History

*The Language of Students' Expository Writing and Teachers' Expectations*

# Knowing and Writing School History

*The Language of Students' Expository Writing and Teachers' Expectations*

## Luciana C. de Oliveira

*Purdue University*

INFORMATION AGE PUBLISHING, INC.
Charlotte, NC • www.infoagepub.com

KH

**Library of Congress Cataloging-in-Publication Data**

De Oliveira, Luciana C.
 Knowing and writing school history : the language of students' expository writing and teachers' expectations / Luciana C. de Oliveira.
     p. cm.
 Includes bibliographical references.
 ISBN 978-1-61735-336-9 (pbk.) – ISBN 978-1-61735-337-6 (hardcover) – ISBN 978-1-61735-338-3 (e-book)
 1. English language–Composition and exercises–Study and teaching (Secondary) 2. Exposition (Rhetoric)–Study and teaching (Secondary) 3. Historiography–Study and teaching (Secondary) I. Title.
 LB1631.D292 2011
 428.0071–dc22

                                                        2010049816

Printed in the United States of America

4/15/13

# *Dedication*

---

*To my mother, my first teacher,*
*Maria do Carmo de Souza Oliveira,*
*who made my dream become a reality.*

*À minha mãe, minha primeira professora,*
*Maria do Carmo de Souza Oliveira*
*que fez meu sonho tornar-se realidade.*

# Contents

Dedication..................................................................................v

Acknowledgments .................................................................xi

Introduction...........................................................................xiii

**1** Background.............................................................................1

   History: A Literate Discipline .............................................. 1

   History Teaching and Language Needs in California.................. 3

   Methodology and Data Sources............................................. 4

      *Context for the Study* ...................................................... 4

      *Roles of the Researcher* ..................................................... 5

      *Data Sources and Participants*............................................ 6

      *Data Analysis*............................................................... 9

**2** Teaching, Learning, and Writing School History............................. 13

   Teaching and Learning History ....................................... 14

      *Developing Historical Understanding*.................................. 14

      *Making History More than Memorization of "Facts"*.................. 15

      *Learning to Think like Historians*..................................... 15

   Challenges of Teaching History......................................... 16

      *School Reform Efforts* .................................................... 16

      *History as Subject Matter: Text Dependence and Language Demands*... 17

      *Content Coverage*.......................................................... 18

   Writing in History ....................................................... 19

      *Expectations for Historical Writing*.................................... 19

*Historical Understanding Display* ......................................................... 19

*Writing as a Form of Historical Understanding Display* ................... 21

*Expectations for Historical Genres* ...................................................... 23

**3** History Teachers' Challenges and Reported Practices Using
and Teaching Writing ............................................................................. 29

Goals of History as a School Subject ................................................. 30

Challenges in Teaching History: Implications for the
Teaching of School History Writing ................................................ 31

*Themes about Challenges in School History* ..................................... 32

Teachers' Perspectives and Instructional Practices in
Teaching Writing ............................................................................... 41

*Teachers' Perspectives on Writing* ...................................................... 41

*Teachers' Instructional Practices* ........................................................ 43

Discussion and Implications ............................................................. 45

**4** Student Writing in History ................................................................... 49

Teachers' Expectations for the Expository Writing Task ............. 50

Text Analysis and Results ................................................................. 53

Text One ............................................................................................. 54

*Theme and Method of Development* ..................................................... 55

*Elaboration* .......................................................................................... 59

*Logical Relationships* ........................................................................... 62

*Reference* ............................................................................................. 63

The Linguistic Constructs at Work: Text Two ............................. 65

*Summary* ............................................................................................. 73

English Language Learners ............................................................... 74

*Example of an Essay in Need of Improvement* .................................. 74

Example of a Successful Essay: Text Four .................................... 80

Discussion ........................................................................................... 83

*Expectations for the Expository Writing Task* .................................. 83

*Differences Between More and Less Effective Texts* ........................... 84

**5** Student Writing in History ................................................................... 89

Teachers' Expectations for the Expository Writing Task ............. 89

Text Analysis and Results ................................................................. 91

*Example of Successful Essays: An English Speaker and an
English Language Learner* .................................................................. 92

Example of an Essay in Need of Improvement .......................... 116

Discussion ................................................................................. 121

Notes ........................................................................................ 123

**6**   Conclusions and Implications ................................................. 125

Teaching Writing in History ..................................................... 125

The Discipline-specific Nature of School History Writing ........ 127

Accomplishing Goals, Overcoming Challenges: Supporting
History Educators .................................................................. 128

Teaching Development and Analysis in School History:
The Role of Theme, Evaluation, and Elaboration ............... 130

Providing Meaning-Based Feedback ......................................... 134

The Language of History: Developing Students' Literacy
and Historical Understanding ............................................... 135

**A**   Questionnaire .......................................................................... 137

**B**   Interview 1 Questions .............................................................. 141

**C**   Interview 2 Questions .............................................................. 143

References ................................................................................. 145

# *Acknowledgments*

$T$his project could not have been completed without the assistance and support of several people. First, I would like to thank Mary Schleppegrell (University of Michigan), my advisor, mentor, and dissertation chair, for providing support and encouragement in all aspects during the project; for sharing her expertise; for countless hours of guidance, help, and patience; and for her faith in me. I thank Steve Athanases (University of California, Davis) for his mentoring over the years, for helping me theorize about education, and for his careful reading of my writing. I also thank AG Rud (Washington State University) for his suggestions to improve my work and careful reading of my manuscript. Special thanks go to Melanie Shoffner (Purdue University) for her careful proofreading of this book and suggestions to improve it. A special note of gratitude is due my friend and role model Lia D. Kamhi-Stein (California State University, Los Angeles), who continues to encourage, support, and assist me in every way possible. I am honored to have worked with each of them. Thanks also to the production team at Information Age Publishing for making this book possible.

I thank my family for their love and belief in me. Thanks to my mother, Maria do Carmo, for helping and supporting me in every way possible and my brother, Leopoldo, for always being a role model for me since I was a child. My husband, Alex Noguera, has been extremely generous with emotional support throughout this project. Thanks for letting me estar en mi mundo, like he puts it, for so many hours a day so that I could focus on

*Knowing and Writing School History,* pages xi–xii
Copyright © 2011 by Information Age Publishing
All rights of reproduction in any form reserved.

**xi**

my writing. Thanks for reminding me to take a break from writing and for always being there for me when I needed some encouragement.

In addition, I would like to thank the history teachers who participated in this study. In particular, I thank the four focus history teachers, Maggie, Peter, Jerry, and Tom; this project would not have been possible without them. I thank them for agreeing to let me interview them and for spending time with me reading students' essays and telling me about their lives as teachers. I also thank the students whose writing is portrayed here.

Thanks also go to my colleagues and friends who have always been supportive of my work. I thank Camila Höfling, Denise M. de Abreu-e-Lima, and Eliane H. Augusto-Navarro (Federal University of São Carlos) for their continued encouragement. I am also grateful to my colleagues and friends at Purdue University for their continuing support.

Special thanks go to the staff of the History Project at UC Davis and the two school districts from the Sacramento region that provided data for the study. Nancy McTygue in particular was unfailingly supportive of my work.

Finally, I wish to thank the School of Education at UC Davis for the financial support during my Ph.D. program, without which I would not have been able to finish my doctoral degree.

# Introduction

*If we want to help our students learn to read and write better, to comprehend texts*
*in English and to compose texts in English more successfully, we will therefore have to*
*develop, as a complement to our knowledge of the reading and writing processes,*
*a more explicit understanding of what those texts—those products—are like,*
*how they differ from the texts that our students have known, and what uses*
*we typically make of them in our particular discourse communities.*

—David Eskey (1993, p. 231)

## Background

These opening words, by internationally renowned literacy scholar David
Eskey (1993), provide the impetus for the focus of this book. As Eskey highlights, we must develop a more explicit understanding of the characteristics
of different texts as products and how they are used in particular discourse
communities. This book addresses this by focusing on the written products
of students in 8th and 11th grades in the discourse community of school
history. In this study, I identify the linguistic challenges that students face
as they engage in academic tasks that require advanced levels of reading
and writing in secondary history classes. As a result, I provide pedagogical
implications and suggestions for teacher education and for the professional
development of history teachers by suggesting ways to work with language
as a means of helping students learn history in secondary school. The data
set consists of writing done by students who were English language learners and other culturally and linguistically diverse students from two school
districts in California. The book is an investigation of expository school

*Knowing and Writing School History,* pages xiii–xviii
Copyright © 2011 by Information Age Publishing
**xiii**

history writing and teachers' expectations for this type of writing. *School history writing* is used here to refer to the kind of historical writing expected of students at the pre-college levels.

Researchers in the area of history pedagogy contend that students should be explicitly taught how to write different kinds of texts (McCarthy, Young, & Leinhardt, 1998; Voss & Wiley, 2000). The research community provides some guidance for history teachers (e.g., Leinhardt, 2000), but more information is needed about the characteristics of the writing that is expected from students in higher grades and how teachers can support and scaffold writing development in history. Despite teachers' lack of expertise in this area, all students, English language learners (ELLs) and native speakers alike, are expected to show their knowledge and understanding of history, and writing is the major form of evaluation of such understanding. No research study to date has investigated the intersection between teachers' expectations for school history writing, analysis of student writing in history, and the reported impediments for a focus on writing in history. The present study fills this gap in investigations of student writing and teachers' expectations and practices in the content area of history. The study analyzes the expository writing produced by students in 8th and 11th grades and investigates the language features that are most significant for the development of their ideas.

## The Need for an Investigation of Language Demands and Expectations in School History

Because history often relies on reading and writing and has its own discipline-specific challenges, it is important to understand the language demands of this content area, the typical writing requirements, and the language expectations of historical discourse. History uses language is specialized ways, so it can be challenging for students to construct responses to historical facts and events. It is only through a focus on these specialized ways of presenting and constructing historical content that students will see how language is used to construe particular contexts. Historical thinking demands students' realization of connections, relationships, and interpretations. Students need to be able to write texts in order to make these connections, build relationships, and construct interpretations. Because of students' language needs, they need language support in history in order to be successful in these tasks.

When students write history texts, they can be made aware of discourse features that express different meanings. Students must understand that every text a historian writes is an interpretation in itself. Students must also recognize that the texts presented at school are a compilation of explanations. Historians do not just record what happened; they interpret and explain, and this involves the presentation of social values and different points of view (Martin & Wodak, 2003). Students of school history are also expected to develop interpretations and demonstrate their historical understanding through writing and often need to present opposing viewpoints to show their understanding of a debate, an important movement, a time period, and historical events. When students need to take a position on a certain issue, for example, they need to consider the multiple perspectives on the issue before they can assess. This involves considering the multiple voices of history, which requires presenting different sides of an issue. This study shows that presenting these multiple voices is particularly important in responding to an expository writing task.

Many junior high and high school history teachers find the teaching of writing challenging. They frequently report their lack of time to focus on writing and to show students how to organize their thoughts by preparing them to write in history. Students seldom know teachers' expectations and goals for writing. Yet students are expected to show their historical understanding in writing. However, if the teaching of writing is neglected, students may be unable to accomplish writing tasks successfully. Students need greater exposure to and instruction in writing in order to be prepared for further schooling. The research community needs to investigate what students are doing when they write in history and provide more guidance for teachers on how to scaffold writing for students in such a way that is reasonable, considering current content and standards requirements. In addition, the kinds of requirements and expectations for history learning need to be investigated. As Eskey (1993) puts it,

> [T]o better understand ourselves as teachers, we must also find answers to such questions such as these: what is it that we want our students to do, or be able to do, in their reading and writing? How can we induce them to adopt and implement this particular approach to the value and uses of literacy? (p. 227)

This means that we must understand what our expectations are for students in their reading and writing. Because reading and writing are so important for students' understanding of history, these questions are key and need to be further explored.

These issues were evident to me in my own work with the California History–Social Science Project (CH–SSP). My experience with the History Project at the University of California–Davis sparked my interest in these issues and enabled me to investigate them in more detail. A literacy focus was added to the project in order to address educational issues noted in the state of California: an increasing number of ELLs, many students' low literacy scores, a high number of classroom teachers with emergency credentials, and increasing standards-based instruction initiatives. As one of the program literacy leaders at the History Project (HP) from UC–Davis from 2002 until 2006, I had firsthand experience with the challenges of history discourse faced by students. The area of writing instruction was particularly salient due to the discipline-specific nature of writing in history, where students are expected to present an interpretation and support it with historical information. I became interested in how writing is used in history classes and wanted to investigate how students respond to certain writing tasks. Specifically, I wanted to examine the grammatical and lexical resources used by students in middle and high school to construct an exposition.

## Overview of the Book

In order to help students increase their linguistic potential, we need to understand not only the expectations for their writing but also what it is they are doing with language when writing history texts, that is, how they are using language to demonstrate their understanding of history. Without such emphasis on the actual features of students' writing, advice on how to help students develop their language skills and increase their achievement in history can only be given based on assumptions about what constitutes "good writing," assumptions that often call on notions such as "clarity" and "elaboration"—and teachers often have no clear understanding of how these abstract notions are realized in language. I provide specific history-related recommendations for how teachers can focus effectively on language in teaching students to write school history and provide guidance for teachers on how to scaffold writing for students in a way that responds to current content and standards requirements.

This study is situated within discipline-based conceptions of writing in which literate activities are seen as processes and acts embedded within specialized discourse communities that value particular ways of acting, writing, and talking (Christie, 2002; Gee, 2002). Little is known about the expectations for students' writing in history classes and the language resources that students use when they write to demonstrate their historical knowledge. Bringing these areas together in a study enables us to gain insight into a more complete view of historical literacy. This investigation informs professional development leaders of students' language needs and teachers' expectations for what students should be achieving in school history writing. With this information, policies, practices, and programs can be modified or created to address the needs of students in history classes. Appropriate interventions based on a more complete understanding of students' writing can be conceptualized and put into practice.

Functional linguistic research in Australia has demonstrated that there are significant differences in terms of the grammatical resources used by students when writing at different points in their schooling (Coffin, 1997; 2004) and in different content areas (Martin, 2002; Unsworth, 1999). I am able to further this work by focusing on students in California in middle-school (8th-grade) and high-school (11th-grade) history by identifying resources needed for school success in history and showing whether and how these resources differ as students move from middle to high school in U.S. History classes.

The overall goal of the study is to investigate the language resources that 8th- and 11th-grade students draw on to write an exposition. Another goal is to consider the role of writing in school history and how writing is taught in history classrooms. One particularly important aspect of this book is that it combines linguistic analyses of student writing with educational considerations in the under-researched content area of history. This interdisciplinary approach to studying writing and teaching practice is particularly relevant for what it can show about student writing. This approach helps identify writing areas that can be a focus in history classes to help further students' historical understanding and its demonstration through language.

## Research Questions

This book addresses these issues by answering the following research questions: (1) How is writing used and taught in 8th- and 11th-grade history classes in two school districts in California? (2) What are the expectations for students' writing in history? (3) What are the language features that enable students to write the expository genre at the 8th- and 11th-grade levels in school history? (4) What skills do 8th- and 11th-grade students need to reach the level they are expected to reach? I draw on questionnaire data from 44 history teachers who have attended History Project events, interviews with four focus history teachers from two school districts in Sacramento, and essay data from these four teachers' classes, and I conduct a linguistic analysis of 8th- and 11th-grade student essays using the theoretical framework of systemic–functional linguistics. This linguistic theory allows me to examine these texts in terms of the particular language and organizational choices of writers that construct the meanings within a text. It further enables the investigation of how these choices help writers construct the texts in the particular context of writing a historical argument.

### Chapter Summary

Chapter One provides the background, rationale, and method for the study. It specifies the data sources and analysis procedures and gives an overview of the research questions and how they were addressed in the study.

Chapter Two reviews literature in history teaching and learning as well as student writing in history. The chapter begins by identifying some goals and challenges in teaching history. The chapter also highlights the place of writing in school history, identifying some key writing studies in history.

Chapter Three presents the results of interviews and questionnaires with history teachers. It focuses on history teachers' reported challenges and practices using and teaching writing in school history.

Chapter Four presents the analysis of 8th-grade student writing and highlights the major language features of students' essays that enabled them to construct essays that were considered successful or in need of improvement. The chapter also features the writing of mainstreamed ELLs and discusses the linguistic resources they draw on to write.

Chapter Five presents the analysis of 11th-grade student writing, emphasizing the language resources that 11th-grade students employ when they write. The chapter contrasts the 11th- and 8th-grade analysis by highlighting some major differences and similarities between the writing tasks students performed.

Chapter Six presents conclusions and implications of the study for teacher education and professional development.

# 1

## *Background*

History is a subject area that has received special attention in the last few years. History has been investigated by educational psychologists, linguists, and educators interested in how history is constructed and interpreted by students and historians (Wineburg, 1991; 2001), how history students write in school history (Coffin, 1997; 2002; 2004), and how history is learned and historical reasoning and thinking developed (Leinhardt, Stainton, & Virji, 1994; McKeown & Beck, 1994). This body of work is part of a growing field of study to which this book contributes. I investigate expository school history writing and teachers' expectations for this type of writing. *School history writing* refers to the kind of historical writing expected of students at the pre-college levels.

## History: A Literate Discipline

Student understanding of history is highly dependent on reading textbooks and other sources and writing essays to demonstrate knowledge of the content area. Middle and secondary history teachers often report the difficulties of teaching writing in history and feel unprepared to teach writing because they did not receive enough preparation in their credential programs to focus on writing in the subject matter they are teaching.

The content area of history holds the potential to develop students' literacy. Historical content is presented through reading and writing tasks at

*Knowing and Writing School History,* pages 1–11
Copyright © 2011 by Information Age Publishing
All rights of reproduction in any form reserved.

school. In order to successfully participate in this subject area, students must learn to use language in particular ways (Mohan, 1986). The grammatical choices that realize the texts of history are unlike the English language that students use every day in their lives outside of school (Schleppegrell, 2001; 2004). As the concepts students must learn become more difficult at higher grade levels, the grammar that constructs these concepts also becomes more distinctive and specialized.

History requires more than memorization of facts; historical understanding entails making connections between and interpreting the significance of events and movements (Spoehr & Spoehr, 1994; Greene, 1994). History is a specialized form of literate practice and activity (Stodolsky, 1988). The discourse of history has distinctive features since it involves building interpretations and perspectives about historical events, movements, people, and periods (Martin, 2002). As Martin (2002) puts it, "[S]aying why things happened as they did necessarily involves a stance—an evaluative orientation to what is going on" (p. 101). This "evaluative orientation" is especially significant since evaluative meanings are necessary for the development of expository writing of the kind discussed here.

Evaluative meanings have received special attention in studies of history (e.g., Coffin, 2002; Eggins, Wignell, & Martin, 1993; Martin, 2002). These studies have shown that students need to be able to evaluate and analyze historical interpretations. Students need to be able to use evaluation successfully in history writing since much of what students are asked to accomplish in history depends on their ability to evaluate. Construing evaluative meanings is especially relevant for responding to an expository writing task in history, where values and judgments enable the construction of interpretations and perspectives.

One of the main issues that history teachers find with students' essays is the lack of development and organization of ideas. These notions are considered here from a linguistic point of view. Key linguistic resources and strategies that construct "development" and "organization" are identified. The study finds that elaboration of meanings is best described as a set of language resources that enables the kind of development that history teachers typically discuss. Elaboration, in teachers' views, involves students providing historical support for their assertions in the form of examples from historical sources. Teachers claim that students know that they are to provide examples to support their positions, but they do not know how to link the examples to the points developed in their essays or to connect them to their thesis statements. This investigation shows that elaboration is the most distinguishing feature between essays considered "strong" and "weak" and that the elaboration that teachers discuss is realized through the grammatical and lexical choices that students make that enable them to reiterate ideas already presented, expand their points, explore other positions, and specify in more detail by providing examples.

## History Teaching and Language Needs in California

Teachers are faced with many demands in schools today, including working with a linguistically and culturally diverse population with many language needs. Assessments of students in history present a difficult situation. According to the National Assessment of Educational Progress (2001), only 11 percent of 12th-grade students test at or above the proficiency level in historical skills. Included in such skills is the ability to employ historical evidence to support positions and to write arguments that reveal a thorough understanding of issues and that use multiple sources. History is particularly challenging for students with poorly developed academic language and for those who speak English as an additional language.

Many students entering California schools come from non-English speaking backgrounds. In the 2008–2009 academic year, out of the total student enrollment in California schools, English language learners (ELLs) corresponded to 25% of the total student population, that is, 1.5 million students (California Department of Education, 2010). In most classrooms today in California, many ELLs are faced with the linguistic and academic challenges of developing their language. Many ELLs go through ESL or bilingual programs so they can develop a certain level of English proficiency before they are mainstreamed. When ELLs, also referred to as Limited English Proficient (LEP) students, have achieved a certain level of English proficiency (levels 4 and 5 in a scale of 1–5) and are thus considered Fluent English Proficient (FEP), they are mainstreamed and take classes with other ELLs as well as native English speakers. When ELLs are reclassified and mainstreamed, most (if not all) language services and instructional support may be discontinued.

ELLs are not the only ones who need language support. Academic language, "language that stands in contrast to the everyday informal speech that students use outside the classroom environment" (Bailey & Butler, 2002, p. 7), is a "second" language for all students. The kind of language students learn at school is different from ordinary language for communicative purposes (Schleppegrell, 2001; 2004). Academic English is generally learned in school from teachers and textbooks, and only with proper instructional support (Fillmore & Snow, 2000; Schleppegrell, 2004). Knowledge about how academic language differs from ordinary language is critical for teachers who are preparing students for higher levels of schooling.

In addition, a key aspect for teachers is knowledge about how discourses of a specific discipline differ from those of other disciplines. Every discipline uses academic language in specific ways (Schleppegrell, 2004). These differences have to do with the nature of the discipline itself. History has its own expectations and typical discipline-specific linguistic choices that present and re-present historical interpretations and perspectives. This specificity makes the discourse of history particularly challenging.

## Methodology and Data Sources

### Context for the Study

**The History Project**

Part of the California History–Social Science Project (CH–SSP), the History Project (HP) from UC Davis, working primarily with the Sacramento region school districts, has offered programs with a standards-based historic content and curriculum focus since 1991, when the HP was established. Monthly sessions and a summer institute focusing on teaching American history have been offered by the project for eight years. Facing challenges in teaching students from diverse backgrounds and developing standards-based curriculum, history teachers have reported the need to strengthen their strategies and increase student achievement in history.

By providing models of curricula that integrate literacy and content development, the HP literacy program focuses on discipline-specific literacy strategies. Working with the non-simplified, complex language of history as it is used in actual adopted textbooks and other sources, participants learn to apply these strategies by analyzing texts and developing their own curricula. The goal of the literacy institute is to help assure that all students, both monolingual English speakers with low literacy skills and ELLs, receive instruction that allows them access to and success in history.

The literacy program was designed to address literacy challenges created by primary and secondary sources and to help teachers create curricula that offer text analysis techniques for students in their reading of history texts. This program is a collaborative effort between history teachers and linguists who work together to develop curricula that utilize strategies to increase student literacy. The current "Building Literacy through History" summer workshop uses a combination of functional grammar, language awareness, and writing strategies. The functional grammar component of the literacy program, based on the current systemic–functional linguistic theory, offers ways of looking at how the language of history is constructed in texts and at alternatives for deconstructing such language. Attention to reading is an important component since understanding reading materials and texts of different kinds becomes gradually more significant in education as students become older (Kress, 1997; Wells, 2002).

The writing program of the literacy institute focuses on the argument genre and considers the ability to write in such a genre evidence of advanced literacy. Based on Coffin's (1997) work on the genres of history and Jane Schaffer's (1995) English Language Arts writing program adapted to history, the writing program addresses several components of an argument, such as writing thesis statements in history, writing introductions and conclusions, and using evidence and examples in history arguments.

The HP is constantly in the process of evaluating its various programs. As part of the evaluation efforts, data were collected from two school districts in Sacramento in 2005–2006. The purpose of the evaluation is to provide a detailed assessment of the impact of professional development provided by the HP.

The two school districts that provided data for this study are Districts 1 and 2. These districts are not named here because of confidentiality issues. District 1 serves a racially and ethnically diverse student population of over 12,000 K–12 students, with a high number of Hispanic (21%), African American (19%), and Asian (13%) students. District 2 is among the 10 largest school districts in California, serving about 50,000 K–12 students. The district's largest student population is Hispanic (29%), with 23% Asian, 22% African American, and 22% White.

## Roles of the Researcher

My main duties with the HP included development of curricula that integrate literacy strategies in history for the summer literacy institute and year-round guidance in the application of different literacy strategies by history teacher-leaders working with the HP. During the summer literacy institute, I presented literacy strategies integrated in history lessons and worked one-on-one with teachers to assist them in incorporating literacy strategies in their own lessons. I also assisted in statewide efforts to infuse such strategies in professional development for history teachers throughout the state. I have worked with history teacher leaders and program coordinators from UC Berkeley, UCLA, UC Irvine, CSU Fresno, and CSU Chico. I wanted to know more about the specific challenges that historical texts posed to English learners and at-risk students.

---

## Data Sources and Participants

The present research study involved a number of data sources and participants. Since I worked with the HP for three years, I developed a network that I was able to tap into for this study. The data sources for this project included questionnaires, teacher interviews, and student writing in history. In order to learn expectations of student writing in history, I collected questionnaire data from 44 history teachers from the Sacramento region, four of whom were interviewed (two 8th-grade teachers and two 11th-grade teachers). This enabled me to address my second research question by describing what current history teachers identify as expectations for students' writing. The teachers I interviewed are currently teaching at two different, low-performing school districts in Sacramento with which the HP is currently working. These teachers represent the diversity of teaching experience, professional preparation, and professional involvement with the HP. This enabled me to focus on the teachers' writing expectations in the two grade levels from which student writing data were collected.

It is also important to examine what students are actually doing when they write in history. To investigate what language features enable students to write expected genres at the 8th- and 11th-grade levels in school history, student writing data from the evaluation project were analyzed. To identify what skills 8th- and 11th-grade students need to reach the level they are expected to reach, I compared the analysis of students' writing with the descriptions and identification of expectations for student writing, based on the preliminary and discourse-based interviews. I formulated the expectations I identified in linguistic terms. This allowed me to show what linguistic resources students would need in order to gain control of the literacy demands of history discourse.

### Questionnaires

A questionnaire that focused on the teaching of writing in history (see Appendix A) was sent out through an HP online database to history teachers in the Sacramento region who had participated in HP activities. Forty-four questionnaires were completed. The questionnaire asked teachers to discuss the role of standards in their teaching and the role of writing in history. They were asked to describe two different classes they taught and discuss their assessment practices in the classes. In addition, the questionnaire asked teachers to specify the recurring problems that students face when they write in history. Questionnaire participants ranged from having 2 to 34 years of teaching experience and taught elementary, middle, or high school U.S. History, World History, Geography, or Social Studies.

## Teacher Interviews

Each of the four teachers was interviewed twice by the researcher. The interviews were semi-structured (Merriam, 2002) and included more and less structured questions. The highly structured part of the interview was used to collect specific information needed from all participants (Merriam, 2002). The largest part of the interview was a list of questions and issues.

In the first semi-structured interview, teachers were asked general questions about the teaching of history and about their experiences with the teaching of writing in history (see Appendix B). The second interview was a discourse-based interview in which the teachers and the researcher looked at student writing samples and discussed students' historical knowledge and how their historical understanding was being demonstrated in writing. Each interview was conducted at the school site and lasted at least 70 minutes.

A discourse-based interview was conducted after this preliminary interview. A discourse-based interview has as its main characteristic the focus on written documents. Prior to this second interview, I made copies of a class set of evaluation essays from each of the four teachers, gave them the essays, and asked them to select essays from the class set. Each teacher selected essays based on their assessment of content knowledge displayed and process of writing. Teachers were asked to select at least one essay that they considered in need of improvement on both content and process of writing and one that they evaluated as strong in both the content and process of writing. During the interview, we were able to talk about those essays, why they selected them, and these teachers' expectations for student writing. In this discourse-based interview, I first went through the essay prompt from the HP and asked teachers what their expectations would be for each answer. In other words, teachers were to describe what the best essay would include in terms of content and organization. Each interview was specific to each teacher, but some main questions were common to all interviews (see Appendix C).

Four history teachers from two school districts in the Sacramento region participated in this study. Three of these teachers taught in District 1 and one taught in District 2. All four teachers have participated in HP events at different points in their careers. These teachers are all committed to their profession, based on my own assessment of their participation in HP-related institutes and activities. They represent diversity of teaching experience, professional preparation, and professional involvement with the HP. They attended the literacy program offered by the HP in different years.

Maggie Taylor teaches 10th and 11th grades in District 1. Maggie had taught for 21 years at the time of the study and at 7th, 8th, 10th, and 11th grades in different years throughout her career. She has been teaching

11th-grade U.S. History since 1999 and Advancement Placement History since 2003. She holds a bachelor's degree in Spanish and a teaching credential in Language and History.

Peter Russell teaches 10th and 11th grades in District 2. Peter had taught for 20 years at the time of the study and taught all subjects in 6th, 7th, and 8th grades from 1985 until 1995. He then moved to his current school district and taught history to 10th, 11th, and 12th grades. From 2002 until 2004, Peter taught World History and Advancement Placement World History. He has taught Advancement Placement U.S. History and Advancement Placement World History since 2004. His bachelor's degree is in History and his teaching credential is in Social Studies.

Tom Marble teaches 8th grade in District 1. Tom had taught Physical Science for four years when he started teaching U.S. History in 2001. In 2002–2004, Tom also taught a 7th-grade corrective reading program. Tom has a bachelor's degree in Government and Environmental Studies and a teaching credential in Social Studies and Introductory Science.

Jerry Michaels is an 8th-grade teacher in District 1 and has been teaching 8th-grade U.S. History for 5 years. His bachelor's degree is in Music and his teaching credential in Social Studies.

Information on these participants' teaching experience is presented in Table 1.1.

### Essays

In order to understand the language features that enable students to write at the 8th- and 11th-grade levels in school history, I conducted a linguistic analysis of essays from 8th- and 11th-grade students collected for the UCD HP's evaluation study. After a preliminary interview with the four focal teachers, each teacher was given a class set of essays, from which each teacher selected essays based on their assessment of content knowledge displayed and process of writing. This student writing corpus consisted of a total of 63 essays, 24 from 8th grade and 39 from 11th grade. Teachers were

**TABLE 1.1  Teaching Information on Focus Teachers**

| Teacher | Grade | Years Teaching | Years with District |
|---------|-------|----------------|---------------------|
| Maggie | 10th and 11th | 21 | 16 |
| Peter | 10th and 11th | 20 | 5 |
| Tom | 8th | 4 | 4 |
| Jerry | 8th | 5 | 5 |

asked to select at least one essay that they considered in need of improvement on both content and process of writing and one that they evaluated as strong on both the content and process of writing. I then analyzed the essays that each of my focal teachers selected from their own class sets. This corpus consisted of 26 essays, 14 8th-grade and 12 11th-grade essays.

## Data Analysis

### Questionnaires

Each question was analyzed individually across all completed questionnaires and emerging themes and issues were identified. Questions 4, 5, 6, 7, and 8 were analyzed in detail to show current practices in using and teaching writing by teachers. These questions focused on the role of writing in history and whether and how writing has been addressed in history classes.

Data analysis was simultaneous with data collection in order to maintain and sharpen the research focus, to prevent repetition, and to keep control of the database (Merriam, 1998). Analysis followed the constant comparative method (Merriam, 1998), which involves a constant comparison of one unit of data with another, comparison of new data to existing codes, organization of emerging concepts into categories, and comparison of units of data with emerging conceptual categories (Merriam, 1998; Strauss, 1987).

Data were coded and recoded according to the constant comparative method until themes began to emerge. A set of rigorous coding procedures guided the analysis to develop theoretically informed interpretations of the data. Strauss (1987) outlines three levels of coding necessary to arrive at core categories that are central relative to other categories, appear frequently in the data, and relate easily to other categories. The first level, initial "open" coding, produced emerging concepts that seemed to fit the data. This is an initial analysis of the data for relevance, suitable category placement, and what is being revealed in the data. The second level, axial coding, uncovered relationships between categories and subcategories. This stage of coding is an intense examination of one category at a time. At this stage, associations with categories that will eventually be selected as core are being made. The third level, selective coding, is a systematic stage of coding and delimits coding to only those codes that significantly relate to core categories. Using these techniques, I identified the expectations teachers have about student writing and was able to show how different informants think about them.

**Teacher Interviews**

Each interview was audiotaped and subsequently transcribed and analyzed. After each interview was transcribed, a preliminary data analysis was done (Merriam, 1998). First, all eight transcripts, totaling 120 double-spaced pages, were reviewed. Second, each interview was carefully read several times. Recurrent issues were identified through these multiple readings. Then, emerging categories and themes were identified and noted. Next, the recurrent issues that had been previously identified in individual interviews were cross-checked across the various interviews.

**Essays**

The evaluation study essays were analyzed using the theoretical framework of systemic–functional linguistics (SFL). SFL is a rigorous method of textual analysis and a theoretically coherent instrument used by several researchers in the field of linguistics and education. This linguistic theory was chosen to analyze the data because it emphasizes how writers' particular language choices construct the meanings within a text (Halliday, 1994) and highlights how social contexts influence textual realizations. This theory allowed me to carry out a textual analysis by examining these student texts in terms of the particular language and writers' organizational choices and how these choices help them construct the texts in particular contexts. A functional analysis focuses on lexico-grammatical features and their realization of particular social contexts. We can look at texts to understand what is happening, who is taking part—as well as their roles and relationships—and what part the language is playing. In order to address my fourth research question, I utilized a combination of procedures. First, I compared the results of the analysis of 8th- and 11th-grade students' writing with the descriptions and identification of expectations for student writing. Looking at what students are actually doing with language when they write and what they are expected to accomplish enables the demonstration of how students are coping with the linguistic demands of history and what other skills are needed for them to be more full participants in the discourse community of history.

Table 1.2 provides an overview of this project's research questions, data sources, and outcomes. This table shows the four research questions that guided this book, the data sources analyzed, and the outcomes of the data analysis. These data sources enabled me to address the research questions by showing that teachers use writing in history in a variety of ways and that students draw on a number of different linguistic resources, depending on the writing task to which they are responding. These differences offer important considerations for professional development and teacher education, as will be shown in Chapters Four and Five.

**TABLE 1.2   Outline of Research Design**

| Research Question | Data Analyzed | Outcomes |
|---|---|---|
| How is writing used and taught in 8th- and 11th-grade history classes in two school districts in California? | • Questionnaires with 44 history teachers from the Sacramento region <br> • Interviews (preliminary) with 4 focal teachers (2 8th-grade, 2 11th-grade) from the Sacramento region | • Description of current practices in writing in school history |
| What are the expectations for students' writing in history? | • Interviews (preliminary and discourse-based) with 4 focal teachers (2 8th-grade, 2 11th-grade) from the Sacramento region | • Description of what history teachers identify as expectations for students' writing in history |
| What are the language features that enable students to write an exposition at the 8th- and 11th-grade levels in school history? | • 24 8th-grade essays <br> • 39 11th-grade essays | • Application of systemic–functional linguistic analysis to student writing to identify linguistic features that students are using in their writing |
| What skills do 8th- and 11th-grade students need to reach the level they are expected to reach? | • Analysis of 8th- and 11th-grade students' writing <br> • Descriptions and identification of expectations for students' writing in history | • Comparison of analysis of 8th- and 11th-grade students' writing with the descriptions and identification of expectations |

# 2

## *Teaching, Learning, and Writing School History*

Teaching, learning, and writing school history is a complex topic that has not been analyzed in depth. Studies that combine issues in teacher education, the preparation of teachers to deal with writing in school history, history teachers' expectations for student writing, and textual analysis of history essays have not specifically been the focus of research. Because there are no studies that examine all of these areas, it is appropriate to examine the literature that focuses on issues in history teaching, history learning, and student writing in history. The research base in history teaching, history learning, and student writing in history has identified goals and challenges of teaching history and has investigated student writing in history. These goals include developing students' historical understanding and knowledge of history (Carretero, & Voss, 1994; Downey & Levstik, 1991; Halldén, 1986, 1998; Leinhardt, Beck, & Stainton, 1994; Stearns, Seixas, & Wineburg, 2001; Wineburg, 2001), making history more than memorization of "facts" (Leinhardt, Stainton, Virji, & Odoroff, 1994), and learning to think like historians (Wineburg & Wilson, 1991).

Writing has received special attention in recent research in the area of history pedagogy. Researchers argue that students need to be explicitly taught how to write different kinds of texts (McCarthy Young & Leinhardt, 1998;

*Knowing and Writing School History,* pages 13–27

Voss & Wiley, 2000). Historical reports, summaries of events and movements, and essays have been identified as some of the writing tasks students are expected to complete in history (Britt, Rout, Georgi, & Perfetti, 1994; Greene, 1994). The number one expectation for students' writing is that they "take a stance" or "make an argument" (Stockton, 1995). *Argument* is a symbol of good writing and is often problematic for students, yet it is one of the most advanced and important text types for students to develop (Greene, 1994; Leinhardt, 2000; McCarthy Young & Leinhardt, 1998; Mitchell & Andrews, 1994; Voss & Wiley, 2000).

## Teaching and Learning History

Studies in history have focused on how to improve history teaching and learning (Beck & McKeown, 1994; Stearns, Seixas, & Wineburg, 2000; Voss & Wiley, 2000). A review of the literature on history learning and teaching (e.g., Carretero & Voss, 1994; Downey & Levstik, 1991; Voss & Wiley, 2000; Wineburg, 1994, 2001) suggests that there is more to learn about students' development of historical understanding, particularly as it relates to students' ability to demonstrate their knowledge in writing.

### *Developing Historical Understanding*

In history, content knowledge involves students' ability to develop historical thinking and understanding, a major goal of history teaching and learning. In recent years, history educators have been interested in history learning and the nature of students' historical understanding and often recognize the importance of reasoning with historical content in history (Downey & Levstik, 1991; Levstik & Pappas, 1992; Voss & Wiley, 2000; Wineburg, 1994, 2001). Reasoning in history can be conceptualized as "the process by which central facts (about events and structures) and concepts (themes) are arranged to build an interpretive historical case" (Leinhardt, Stainton, Virji, & Odoroff, 1994, p. 134). Reasoning and understanding involve knowledge of a given object, issue, event, or person as well as knowledge of conditions and causes related to particular events and require analysis, synthesis, and interpretations of historical phenomena (Leinhardt, Stainton, Virji, & Odoroff, 1994; McCarthy Young & Leinhardt, 1998; Voss & Wiley, 2000). Historical thinking and understanding, according to Wineburg (2001), is not a "natural process," or something that comes automatically with years of schooling.

Part of students' historical understanding is their ability to comprehend historical events through causal relationships. Students need to engage in causal reasoning and to recognize causal connections, fundamental aspects for history learning and understanding (Leinhardt, 2000; Pretorius, 1996; Voss, Carretero, Kennet, & Silfies, 1994). Causality and its expression in historical texts are seen as fundamental for the construction of history discourse (Britt et al., 1994; Coffin, 2004; Halldén, 1986; Perfetti, Britt, Rouet, Georgi, & Mason, 1994; Schleppegrell, Achugar, & Oteiza, 2004; Voss et al., 1994).

## Making History More than Memorization of "Facts"

Helping students go beyond memorization of dates and events to critical analysis and interpretation of recurring themes, issues, ideas, events, institutions, and structures is another important goal of history teaching and learning (Leinhardt, Stainton, Virji, & Odoroff, 1994; McCarthy Young & Leinhardt, 1998). Students often understand that studying history means memorizing facts in chronological order (Spoehr & Spoehr, 1994). According to VanSledright (1997), the National Standards for United States History require much more than memorization and recall of information from a history textbook; they require students to conduct research, analyze, and interpret historical data as well as grapple with historical issues and problems. As VanSledright (1997) puts it, "[S]tudents would learn the 'what' of history (as school district guidelines require), and they would also be engaged in the 'how' and 'why' of history" (p. 3). Brophy (1992) claims that the goal of history instruction is to "go beyond memorizing miscellaneous content by teaching students integrated understandings of networks of related content…" (p. 142).

## Learning to Think like Historians

Another goal for teaching school history is helping students learn to think like historians. Recent work has investigated what historians do when they read, write, and consider history (Greene, 1994; Leinhardt, Stainton, & Virji, 1994). To do history, historians draw inferences based on historical evidence for interpretation (Greene, 1994); build interpretive structures by stepping back from their own initial interpretation and searching for a deeper understanding of issues (Wineburg & Fournier, 1994); and consider historical documents as a corpus of evidence, not as isolated units (Wineburg, 1994), while using different kinds of historical interpretive strategies (Wineburg & Wilson, 1991). Learning to think like historians implies being able to use some of the same methods and approaches that historians use when they examine historical documents and make sense of history.

## Challenges of Teaching History

While recent research has established some goals for history, it has also emphasized the challenges faced by teachers and students in school history classrooms.

### School Reform Efforts

The role of history in schools has been a topic of debate in recent reform efforts. These efforts have been motivated by the low performance of history students on national standardized tests such as the National Assessment of Educational Progress (NAEP) in history (Lapp, Grigg, and Tay-Lim, 2002) and have included a growing emphasis on accountability and standards. Improvement of history education has been at the center of the reform movement, including the Bradley Commission on History in the Schools, the National Standards movement, and reform efforts in a number of individual states (Downey & Fischer, 2000).

These reform efforts, along with an increasingly diverse student population, have placed high demands and challenges on history teachers in particular. According to the National Council for the Social Studies (2004) standards, the primary purpose of the social studies is helping "young people develop the ability to make informed and reasoned decisions for the public good as citizens of a culturally diverse, democratic society in an interdependent world" (Introduction). Yet the content area of social studies is not an emphasis in recent legislations. For example, Burroughs, Groce, and Webeck (2005) investigated the impact of the *No Child Left Behind* (NCLB) legislation on the teaching of social studies in three U.S. states. They found that the legislation emphasizes the development of standards and assessment systems in reading, mathematics, and science, and leaves out other core subjects, such as history and other areas of social studies. The study concludes that many social studies educators are hesitant to request the addition of social studies in NCLB, even though they are unhappy with its omission from the legislation. The social studies educators investigated in the study accepted that attention to this content area will only be provided if federal or state assessments call attention to it. As Burroughs, Groce, and Webeck (2005) put it,

> High school social studies teachers find themselves in the unenviable position of teaching not only a subject that students will come to with a lack of basic skills and understanding, but also one that, seemingly, the "system" dictates that students do not need to learn in the same ways or at the same levels they need to learn reading, mathematics, and science. (p. 19)

In this context of reform efforts and increasing need for teachers, history teachers in particular are required to develop standards-based curricula, deal with the needs of a highly diverse student population, and provide instruction in a number of areas.

## History as Subject Matter: Text Dependence and Language Demands

Student learning in history is highly dependent on reading texts. History textbooks have been under scrutiny by researchers of student learning in history (Beck & McKeown, 1994). Some argue that they do not develop a clear and logical chain of events, making it difficult for students to make connections between events and ideas (McKeown & Beck, 1994) and master the subject matter (Beck, McKeown, Sinatra, & Loxterman, 1991). Studies of history textbooks have examined reading strategies students need to employ to make sense of history textbooks (Harniss, Dickson, Kinder, & Hollenbeck, 2001; Hennings, 1993; Paxton, 1999) and investigated textbooks' strengths and weaknesses (Chambliss, 1994; Kinder, Bursuck, & Epstein, 1992; Tyson & Woodward, 1989). Textbooks are seen as the major type of historical discourse students are exposed to in school history (Ravitch & Finn, 1987; Thornton, 1991). It has been argued that social studies textbooks have had a great influence on the education curriculum, more than any other factor (Kachaturoff, 1982). In fact, Tyson and Woodward (1989) maintain that the textbook is the organizing device of 75% to 90% of all classroom instruction in different subject areas, showing the importance of textbooks in education. A recent study on student learning from textbooks reports that a textbook-centered history curriculum is the reality of many classrooms today (Paxton, 1999). This should not be ignored by educators concerned with the teaching of history in schools.

In their study of an elementary history textbook series, Beck and McKeown (1994) found that history textbooks that students encounter in history classes do not provide appropriate accounts of history. They observed that this inadequacy caused a major problem for elementary teachers, who may lack sufficient content knowledge to fill in the information lacking in the textbook presentation of historical events. Beck, McKeown, and Gromoll (1989), in their investigation of 4th- and 5th-grade social studies programs, found significant variations in curricula, which in turn leads to significant variations in student learning of different content. Textbooks analyzed showed little connection of ideas or events, failed to demonstrate that some ideas were especially important for understanding a topic, did not succeed in making meanings explicit, and provided inadequate explanations.

A number of studies have made an attempt to produce more interesting history textbooks by adding vivid language and captivating details, but these additions did not necessarily lead to superior text comprehension (Paxton, 1999). Despite the apparent inadequacies of history textbooks, they still constitute a major part of the history curriculum and most history teachers use them to support student learning in history. Because textbooks are a highly used resource in history classes, students need to be able to read and understand them to be successful in school history. Being able to access the language used by textbook authors and historians is highly linked to the development of content knowledge and understanding (Harniss et al., 2001), a goal of history teaching.

While recent research has focused on improving textbook language to make it more accessible to students, history discourse in general constitutes a major problem for students due to its language density. Research has shown that reading and writing are regular activities in history that pose serious challenges to students (Schleppegrell, 2004; Schleppegrell, Achugar, & Oteiza, 2004). If the language of history is so challenging for students, Sizer's (2004) conclusion that history is the most difficult subject to teach well in high school is no surprise.

### Content Coverage

One of the major challenges facing history teachers is content coverage (van Hover & Yeager, 2004; Newmann, 1991). Because of the current state of the social studies disciplines, students are exposed to a wide variety of topics (Newmann, 1991). Therefore, coverage of material becomes a major part of history teaching.

Focusing on the disciplines of English literature, biology, and history, Langer (1992) demonstrates, through a report of interviews with teachers, an explicit interest in students' development of higher order thinking skills such as argument. Langer notes that teachers' predominant concern for content is the driving force of curriculum and the examinations students take. Depth versus coverage presents a dilemma for history teachers that is not simply solved (Newmann, 1988; 1991).

School reform efforts, with an emphasis in content areas other than history; features of history as a subject matter, such as text dependence and language demands; and content coverage present challenges for the teaching and learning of history, making it difficult to accomplish the goals for history that recent research has identified. A related area that has been highlighted by history researchers is writing.

## Writing in History

### Expectations for Historical Writing

Writing in history has discipline-specific features (Langer, 1992). However, disciplinary expectations are often not articulated by faculty and teachers (Ball, Dice, & Bartholomae, 1990; Langer, 1992). As a result, the apprentice writer may be left with assumptions and misguided advice on writing practices that appear to be part of the academic discipline (Stockton, 1995). Focusing her research on disciplinary expectations for history, Stockton (1995) observed the apparent gaps between history professors' expectations for student writing and the explicit expression of those expectations for students. After examining interview data with 13 college professors, graded student writing, and relevant course syllabi, Stockton found that professors' assignments explicitly or implicitly called for a thesis, but the resulting student compositions were not always argumentative. Grading and evaluative comments illustrated the importance of organization of information around cause and effect. History teachers, Stockton argues, must make their disciplinary expectations and purposes clear to students; without them, students are likely to continue to fail to comprehend what should be accomplished in their writing. Stockton's research clarifies the potential significance of comprehending college history professors' expectations for students' writing, but because her research does not focus on school history teachers' expectations, little is known about this area.

### Historical Understanding Display

Although the issue of developing students' historical understanding constitutes one problem, a second, related problem is introduced when the issue of students' display of such understanding is considered. Disciplinary knowledge involves knowledge of both content and rhetoric, two important dimensions for the development of disciplinary academic literacy (Langer, 1992; Stockton, 1995, Wineburg, 1991; McCarthy Young & Leinhardt, 1998). Disciplinary knowledge demonstration is fundamental for students at all ages (Stockton, 1995; Wineburg, 1991, 2001).

Langer (1992) emphasizes the centrality of disciplinary knowledge display: "Students must learn, then, not only the basic facts around which discussion is structured but the appropriate and inappropriate ways in which those facts can be presented in the forum defined by that classroom" (p. 71). In order for students to be able to use "appropriate ways" for presenting their ideas, they need to know what those ways are. Langer's words show the key role language plays in students' demonstration of their disciplinary understanding.

Displaying disciplinary knowledge appropriately involves being able to use language features that enable the interpretation of history. Providing examples from history, Schleppegrell (2006) found that expository writing tasks that present claims, evidence, and judgments in authoritative ways are challenging for students. Expectations of history discourse include the demonstration of knowledge through the presentation of historical events in authoritative and structured ways that enable explanation and interpretation (Schleppegrell, 2004).

Through a comparative case study, Monte-Sano (2008) examined two high school history teachers' practices with regards to their students' learning outcomes of writing evidence-based essays. Despite the same average amount of assigned reading and writing, these two teachers had their distinguished perspectives on historical teaching and writing; one aimed to improve her students' abilities to support arguments with evidence, whereas the other was more interested in his students' performance on the Advanced Placement exam and saw summary of factual detail as the key to historical writing. The researcher examined the essays written by 42 students from these two classes participating in pre- and post-assessments of their historical learning and writing over 7 months. Essays were judged on the argumentation and historical reasoning criteria of the Development Rubric of Evidence-Based Historical Writing, which had been designed and refined by the researcher and three history education experts. The purpose of the analysis was to research what kind of teaching would foster growth in evidence-based historical writing.

Based on the comparisons of pre-test and post-test argumentation and reasoning scores obtained by the students from the two classes, Monte-Sano proposes that the teacher's practices focusing on students' abilities to support arguments with evidence offer promise for growth in evidence-based historical writing. Monte-Sano suggests the need for high school history teachers to design tasks, assignments, activities, and readings more consistent with the interpretative aspects of history and to support students with more opportunities to think in terms of evidence. Analysis of the classroom observations and interviews with the teachers gives insights to some particular qualities of reading and writing opportunities that develop students' ability to write evidence-based essays: approaching history as evidence-based interpretation; reading historical texts and considering them as interpretations; supporting reading comprehension and historical thinking; putting students in the role of developing interpretations and supporting them with evidence; and using direct instruction, guided practice, independent practice, and feedback to teach evidence-based writing.

### *Writing as a Form of Historical Understanding Display*

Assessment of content is done through language (Leung, 2001). While multiple-choice items in a history exam require students to process information from text, essay writing assignments require students to use language to demonstrate their knowledge and mastery of content. Essay writing is one of the main evaluation measures used in many tests that evaluate students, including the California High School Exit Exam (CAHSEE). Writing is a necessary "vehicle" for organization and presentation of ideas appropriate in a particular academic discipline (Langer, 1992). When students learn to use writing to display their historical understanding, they are being apprenticed into the discipline of history and are in the process of becoming "part of a community of practice" (Lave & Wenger, 1991, p. 29) with specific discourse patterns.

History researchers have focused on the different organizational patterns that students use as they write arguments and have shown the importance of organizational strategies and students' comprehension of historical writing tasks for students' historical understanding display in writing (Greene, 1994; Leinhardt, 2000; McCarthy Young & Leinhardt, 1998). Less focus has been placed on the patterns of language that students draw on in their writing. Greene (1994), for example, studied how college students make use of information from sources as well as their prior knowledge when writing about historical events and how students' strategies differed from or were similar to historians' approaches to the same tasks. Results showed that students interpreted tasks, organized information, and used concepts and ideas from sources differently according to the task. In addition, students and historians showed different interpretations of the writing tasks. McCarthy Young and Leinhardt (1998) analyzed five document-based writing samples of five student writers according to information selection, organization, and connection. Common organizational patterns were found and specific connectors helped construct the type of organizational pattern used by the students. McCarthy Young and Leinhardt also examined students' use of documents and found three main ways students utilized documents: mentioning them, reinstating them, or integrating and interpreting them.

Organizational patterns, including connectors as well as the use of documents, were also analyzed in Leinhardt's (2000) study. Leinhardt analyzed two essays written by one student, Paul. Paul and the other students in his class were asked to write a short essay in which they would utilize evidence from given documents. According to Leinhardt, Paul's first essay followed a specified-list pattern and five-paragraph theme format in which time, place, and causal-list connectors were used. Causal links (e.g., "although," "however," "as a result," "because") helped construct causal relationships and transitions (e.g., "first of all," "secondly," "finally") helped with the temporal organization, but an overall logical argument was missing. Leinhardt reports that Paul's last essay showed a greater mastery of the five-paragraph format. In this essay, Paul combined his knowledge of the essay format with content of the documents as well as his background knowledge on the topic, and the essay structure was more complete and elaborated. Connections were greatly improved and the use and variety of causal links showed Paul's improvement in this area. He was also able to use evidence from the documents by mentioning them and using their content for his own essay. Leinhardt asserts that Paul's improvements were due to his own efforts as well as feedback from his teacher, mainly feedback on spoken explanations, since feedback on writing was not very regular. The analysis of Paul's progress in history content, history writing, and discussions of history showed how textual analysis can facilitate our understanding of "how students and teachers gain command of and control over the rich details of history as well as the intricacies of building and developing a case within it" (Leinhardt, 2000, p. 242). Students often know the words used to connect ideas but are less certain of the underlying relationships between specific concepts and how those relationships should be expressed in writing (Leinhardt, 2000).

Case studies of actual classrooms and connections to students' writing demonstrate how students can be supported in history classes to develop their historical knowledge. We also need to understand the specific language choices that students make that can support their demonstration of historical understanding. Textual resources have a key role in constructing historical discourse, as shown in functionally-oriented research (Coffin, 1997, 2002, 2004; Eggins, Wignell, & Martin, 1993; Martin, 2002; Veel & Coffin, 1996; Unsworth, 1999). While McCarthy Young and Leinhardt's (1998) and Leinhardt's (2000) research studies offer insights into organizational patterns and use of connectors in writing, functional linguistics research studies have demonstrated that other linguistic resources are important for creating cohesive texts (Achugar & Schleppegrell, 2005). Investigations of writing in history can be further complemented and expanded through a functionally oriented linguistic analysis, which offers an integrated view of language use and considers not only textual elements but also dimensions for creating perspective, that is, elements used to appraise, grade, and give value to events and social experiences.

---

### *Expectations for Historical Genres*

From a functional linguistics perspective, different writing tasks represent different *genres* that have particular social purposes. Genre is a key construct of systemic functional linguistics. Genres are staged and purposeful social processes through which a culture is realized in language (Martin & Rothery, 1986). Each genre has particular register features, that is, lexical and grammatical features that realize a particular text type. According to Martin (1985), "Genres are how things get done, when language is used to accomplish them. They range from literary to far from literary forms: poems, narratives, expositions, lectures, seminars, recipes, manuals, appointment making, service encounters, news broadcasts and so on" (p. 250).

Drawing on her functionally-oriented work in school history in Australia, Coffin (1997) describes a trajectory of genres for school history, moving from structuring the past as story to structuring the past as argument. Coffin describes four distinct historical genres, part of this "pathway" of school history, that move from constructing the past as *story*, where concrete events unfold through time, to constructing the past as *argument*, where particular interpretations are organized through text time. These genres include *historical recount, account, explanation*, and *argument*. Exposition, challenge, and discussion are the three genres included under *argument* in Coffin's framework. The pathway moves from narrative to argument genres and becomes increasingly more abstract as students move along it. Narrative (*account, recount*) genres are organized by external time sequences since chains of events are arranged as they progressed in real time. *Explanation* genres are placed between narrative and argument genres. Explanations use cause–consequence sequences to give details about past events. Explanations use causes and consequences as well as events and are organized in "text time by means of a logical scaffold from which an elaboration of causes and consequences unfolds" (Coffin, 1997, p. 217). The main purpose of explanation genres is to explain and analyze the past and the two main types are factorial and consequential explanations. *Argument* genres, in contrast, are organized by internal time, which "allow separate parts of the text to be connected logically and rhetorical sequences to be built up" (Coffin, 1997, p. 225). Argument genres support a particular interpretation of the past. These texts apply analysis and discussion of differing positions and claims, that is, alternative interpretations are presented, analyzed, and discussed. According to Coffin, for students to be successful in school history, they must be in command of the lexico-grammatical choices and text structures that realize argument genres. As Coffin (1997) explains,

The critical distinction between the explanation genres and the three key arguing genres is the foregrounding of the interpretative nature of historical investigation. Unlike explanations, the arguing genres draw attention to the formation of history as a set of interpretations and "doing history" as a process of negotiating with these different interpretations. Reconstructions of the past are therefore presented as hypothesis rather than fact, as possibilities or probabilities that have to be argued for. (pp. 222–223)

According to Coffin, the challenge genre, one of the historical argument genres highly valued in school history, has as its main goal to argue against a commonly held interpretation of the past. Therefore, persuading readers to reject the interpretation given by historians or textbook writers is at the core of this genre. In addition, in order for writers to support their challenge, they must present counter-arguments as well as an alternative interpretation and evidence supporting it.

Coffin (2004) investigated the role of causality in secondary school student writing in history. Coffin conducted an analysis of 38 texts that represented successful genres in secondary school history. Causal explanations are usually found in argument genres embedded in the evidence. Coffin's choice of successful essays was due to the essays' representation of "typical or 'unproblematic' discourse patterns" (2004, p. 267) and demonstration of significant linguistic features for making historical meaning. Coffin chose student texts belonging to each genre representative of secondary school history and analyzed conjunctions, verbs, nouns, and lexical choices as tools to express causality in history. Different grammatical and lexical choices are used to convey causal associations, and clear patterns of such choices come about when students move from "recording the past" to "arguing about the past" (Coffin, 2004, p. 278). A key finding was the increasing number of abstract nominal forms of causality (e.g., *causes, factors, reasons, results, effects*) used in explanatory and argument genres. According to Coffin (2004), analysis and argumentation are more valued than narrative at the high school level.

Drawing on her previous work, Coffin (2006) shows that historical writing involves different genres and lexico-grammatical features. She demonstrates the powerful role of causality as a meaning-making system in historical writing. Through a comprehensive analysis of the texts that students read and write in secondary school history, Coffin shows the role of language in learning and teaching history. Taking a genre-based view of learning, Coffin examines each historical genre and its role in writing about the past. In addition, she identifies the purposes and expectations in terms of time, cause, and evaluation and how they are used in the discourse of history. Table 2.1 presents the historical genres based on Coffin (1997; 2006), Veel and Coffin (1996), and Martin (2002).

**TABLE 2.1   Genres of History: A Learner Pathway**

| Genre | Social Functions | Description | Elements/Phases | Linguistic Features |
|---|---|---|---|---|
| Recount | Establishes a timeline for a historical narrative | A chronological retelling presented as the arbitrary unfolding of events | • Background<br>• Record of events<br>• Deduction | • Sequence of events<br>• Setting in time<br>• 3rd person<br>• Generic participants<br>• Temporal adjuncts (circumstances)<br>• Abstract terms/grammatical metaphor (nominalization)<br>• Past tense |
| Account | Establishes a sequence of events with causal reasoning about inevitability of narrative | A naturalized linear explanation in which a particular sequence of events is explained with causal reasoning | • Background<br>• Account of events | • Causal links<br>• Generic participants<br>• Material processes<br>• Temporal and causal conjunctions<br>• Declarative mood, 3rd person<br>• Simple present<br>• Grammatical metaphor (nominalization)<br>• Causal relationships within the clause |
| Explanation | Explains the factors or circumstances that led to historical events or the consequences of historical events | A justification for causes and consequences of historical events | • Main statement<br>• Sequence of explanations | • Internal organization of factors<br>• Logical sequencing<br>• Simple present<br>• Declarative mood, 3rd person<br>• Generic participants<br>• Grammatical metaphor (nominalization) |
| Argument | Promotes a position or interpretation of events | A persuasive argument that proposes a position or interpretation through a process of analysis and debate with consideration of many positions and arguments | • Thesis<br>• Main points/arguments with evidence<br>• Reinforcement of thesis | • Nominal expressions name arguments<br>• Modality<br>• Markers of contrast, classification, and logical sequence |

This learner pathway identifies the tasks that students are supposed to perform in writing school history genres, moving from a retelling of events and accounting for why things happened to explaining past events and supporting a particular interpretation of events. These tasks become increasingly difficult as students move through school. This progression from retelling events to arguing for particular positions in a learner pathway is based on linguistic principles described in Halliday's (1993) notion of a language-based theory of learning (Martin, 2002).

The term *argument* is used by the History Project (HP) and history teachers in general to refer to the kind of expository essay described by Martin (2002). Expositions, according to Martin, promote a thesis and put forth an interpretation that needs justifying. An exposition is the genre expected from the prompts used by the evaluation study. Exposition will be the term used in this study to describe such writing.

In general, research on historical understanding and its display in writing is limited. We find research studies that focus more on students' use of documents and connectors in writing and others that focus more on descriptions of school writing and the role of causality in the construction of such writing. However, they do not provide a comprehensive account of the language resources students need to control if they are to be successful in school history writing (except for Coffin's work in Australia). It is important that educators understand disciplinary expectations for writing as well as the way students are using writing to demonstrate their historical understanding.

These research studies share some common findings. Several of them point to the importance of argument as a valued school history genre. Students are expected to develop arguments and express their historical understanding in writing. Yet little is known about disciplinary expectations in school history writing. Even when teachers make it clear that students should "take a stance" or "make an argument," students may lack the linguistic resources to be able to accomplish this successfully. We need to understand the expectations for school history writing and what linguistic resources students use when writing history essays to demonstrate their understanding of history. A focus on the actual features of students' writing is fundamental if we are to assist students in their development of content and language skills. Understanding how "taking a stance" or "making an argument" or "arguing a position" are realized in language and the articulation of teachers' expectations in linguistic terms is significant for better guiding students in their writing. However, research studies to date have not fully addressed teachers' expectations and the linguistic resources students draw on when demonstrating their historical understanding in writing.

History students need to have opportunities to become more prepared for schooling and need more guidance from history teachers to be successful in demonstrating and developing their historical knowledge. Just as historical understanding does not grow naturally (Wineburg, 2001), language does not "simply happen" as children grow older. The development of the ability to make texts is dependent on social experience with making texts (Halliday & Hasan, 1989). Students are often asked to demonstrate their historical understanding through language and in writing. Language and knowledge are interconnected. In Halliday's (1993) words, "[L]anguage is the essential condition of knowing, the process by which experience *becomes* knowledge" (p. 94, emphasis in original). It is frequently through language that students demonstrate their understanding of a discipline. Wineburg (2001) claims, "At its heart, historical understanding is an interdisciplinary enterprise, and nothing less than a multidisciplinary approach will approximate its complexity" (p. 52). This study does just that, use multidisciplinary tools, from linguistics and education, to understand how students demonstrate their historical understanding in writing.

In order to accomplish the goals of higher student achievement in history, we need to focus our efforts on investigating both students and teachers. Therefore, the different themes identified in this chapter, the goals and challenges of teaching history and student writing in history, are brought together in the following chapters. History teachers' perspectives on their goals for history teaching and the challenges they face in teaching history in low income, diverse neighborhoods in California are highlighted. History teachers' expectations for student writing in school history and the language features that enable students to write expected genres at the 8th- and 11th-grade levels in school history are identified. Future professional development efforts can be informed by history teachers' perspectives and the language resources history students need to control to be successful. It is only when we have a more complete picture of what knowledge and skills history students need that we will be able to accomplish our goals of providing students with opportunities to succeed in school history.

# 3

## *History Teachers' Challenges and Reported Practices Using and Teaching Writing*

*There is no doubt that literacy has considerable enabling potential,
but much depends on the kinds of texts that learners are exposed to, the way
they are encouraged to respond to those texts, and the kinds of texts they
are expected to compose in particular discourse communities.*

—David Eskey (1993, p. 228)

This chapter presents goals for history that teachers find important, challenges that history teachers face when they address writing in history classes in California, and history teachers' reported practices using and teaching writing in school history. I will highlight several issues. First, teacher responses overwhelmingly emphasized the importance of writing in history; however, there is a discrepancy when we consider teachers' perspectives on the role of writing in history and their emphasis on writing instruction in history classes. There is a need to understand this discrepancy. Second, what goals do teachers hold for the teaching and learning of history? Finally, what challenges do history teachers who work in highly diverse neighborhoods face and how do these challenges affect the teaching of writing in history?

*Knowing and Writing School History,* pages 29–47
Copyright © 2011 by Information Age Publishing
All rights of reproduction in any form reserved.

This book seeks not only to investigate the skills that history students need to be successful in school history writing, but also to identify current practices and perspectives about writing instruction from history teachers. I use questionnaire data from 44 history teachers and interview data from four focus teachers with different levels of teaching experience. The first section highlights goals of history teaching that history teachers hold, helping lay out some purposes for history. The second section explores the challenges of teaching history in California's schools, with a special focus on how these challenges may influence teachers' instructional decisions and the teaching of school history writing in particular. The third section reports on teachers' questionnaire responses to two questions: (1) *What role do you think writing has in a history class, if any?* (2) *Sometimes history teachers provide writing instruction. Has any of your history teaching been something you might call "teaching writing"? Please explain.* The following section, grounded in interview data from focus teachers, is a description of the goals of history as a school subject.

## Goals of History as a School Subject

The focus teachers highlighted some aspects of history as a school subject that are particularly important for them as they go about doing their jobs. Several goals of history teaching and learning are highlighted in the teachers' views.

One of the goals identified was historical sequencing to understand current events. Maggie underscored the importance of historical sequencing and of history in general by saying, "If you don't know what came before, then what happens next makes no sense whatsoever." This indicates the importance of history in today's world. For Peter, the most challenging but important aspect in teaching history is getting students excited about the subject:

> [History] does affect students daily, it affects their choice for president or local actions, things like that, you need to know about that, you need to know the issues behind things or why is one candidate pushing one thing or not pushing another type of deal, where you stand on that spectrum.

In Peter's view, understanding history is an issue of citizenship and being able to make informed decisions. History has a special place in students' lives, as the use of the verb *affect* indicates. Another issue brought up by Peter was getting students to make connections between different time periods or identifying "the same trend or pattern" or "concepts that kind of run through American history." Getting students to find associations is important for Peter and is a major part of his teaching.

Jerry affirmed that it is easier for kids to make connections when they have some historical background on certain topics and events. This has to do with the character of history itself:

> It's that sense that...one's knowledge of history builds upon a lot of prior things and understanding what went on before and how that leads up to now.... So for me it's not only an issue for passing history class but it's an issue of citizenship as well.

For Jerry, historical background is an important aspect of history teaching. Like Maggie, Jerry places significance on historical sequencing and indicates his view of the importance of history in today's world. Like Peter, Jerry considers an understanding of history to be part of good citizenship and to be vital for making informed decisions and understanding the context for current events.

An issue that Tom feels is very important to cover is "differentiating fact and opinion." Tom says that his students have difficulty identifying when they are reading facts and when they are looking at interpretations or generalizations. Tom deems these distinctions important parts of history teaching. For Tom, developing students' ability to differentiate facts and opinions is critical.

Teachers highlighted some important goals for teaching history and illustrated important skills that students can develop by studying history. Goals for history stress the importance of teachers' work on historical sequencing and providing students with knowledge about history so that they can understand current events with a clear vision of what may have led to these events. Another goal is getting students excited about history so that they get motivated to learn more about history, seeing the importance of history in today's world and viewing an understanding of history as an issue of citizenship, so that the students are better prepared to make informed decisions. An additional goal includes helping students learn that history is about interpretation so that they are able to distinguish between facts and opinions and learn to make historical generalizations based on facts. The history classroom provides a unique space where students can develop historical understanding that has implications for their future lives. However, history teachers also identify challenges in meeting those goals, which are the focus of the next section.

## Challenges in Teaching History: Implications for the Teaching of School History Writing

Many history teachers encounter a difficult reality at their schools: the diminished status of history in comparison with other school subjects. This section highlights the challenges that teachers face when they teach history and the implications of these challenges for the teaching of writing in school history. I draw primarily from the interview data with the four focus teachers: Maggie, Peter, Tom, and Jerry. The findings are divided into themes that emerged from the data.

### Themes about Challenges in School History

The interviews and questionnaires were analyzed by identifying recurrent themes. Themes were constituted by phrases in which teachers shared information about their teaching and the challenges they faced or articulated an issue or problem in addressing writing in their classes. A theme was considered recurrent if the issue, problem, or challenge was articulated at least twice in the interviews or questionnaires of a teacher and if it appeared in the interviews or questionnaires of other teachers as well. As the examples demonstrate, some themes were not mutually exclusive, and some statements could fit into more than one theme. Teachers reported challenges and concerns that broadly fit under three themes:

1. *"History doesn't count."* This theme relates to the low status of history as a content area in California.
2. *Students' limited skills and background.* This theme relates to the limited skills students bring to the history classroom. This theme seemed to be particularly important, due to the characteristics of teachers' school districts: low-income, highly diverse communities.
3. *High demands of the history curriculum and the teaching of writing.* This category encompasses the demands of the history curriculum and their implications for the teaching of writing in history. Teachers are expected to deal with institutional pressures to develop standards-based curricula and to prepare students for standardized tests. The teachers in this study were aware of such forces and were particularly wary of how they influence the teaching and learning of history. These expectations have a clear effect on what teachers select to include in their history classes.

The challenges to which teachers drew attention have a direct connection to the classroom and the teaching and learning of history as well as writing instruction. In each of the following sections, I highlight the language that teachers used to assess their situations. In addition, I highlight teachers' juxtapositions of what students cannot do and what they need to do, constructed in teachers' language.

**"History Doesn't Count"**

Teachers highlighted issues related to the low status of history in schools. In Maggie's view, attention to reading and math leads to a problematic reality for the school subject of history and especially for 11th-grade history teachers. Because history is not a major focus in the middle school curriculum, Maggie reported her struggles to try to catch up on several aspects of the curriculum that students should have learned in lower grades:

> We get kids from a junior high who have had little or no U.S. history or World history in the 7th or 8th grade. They've been concentrating on reading and math—sometimes they get one semester of each [i.e., U.S. history and World history], sometimes they get one semester of one or the other, sometimes they get nothing.

Maggie's language shows, through the negative markers *little or no U.S. History or World History* and *nothing*, the lack of students' background in history. Similarly, Peter reports that students see the practicality of other school subjects, such as math, but often do not see the importance of history. His struggle is in helping students see that history needs to be respected, which may be an issue because of the greater institutional value placed on other school subjects, such as math, reading, and science. Peter considers it especially challenging to get students interested in history because, "for most of them and a lot of people in our society, math, and reading and science are the big things—'History doesn't count. I'm not going to be a historian. I'm not going to do history the rest of my life.'" Here we see the language of negation as well. Peter emphasizes that *history doesn't count* from students' perspectives. Peter believes that students bring a certain attitude to the history classroom that is partly due to the status of history in society. According to Peter, many students claim that, because they are not going to be historians or do history after high school, they are not interested in history as a school subject.

Jerry places emphasis on getting his students to "think like historians," looking at the "processes that historians go through when they are trying to find out about the past and what are the thinking habits that they have." Jerry believes that this is very difficult for his students because some are still struggling with finding history an important subject. Jerry, like Peter and Maggie, stresses that,

> a lot of times, students, I think they get the sense that, some of them get a sense that history is not as important as math and language arts. In fact, I

think sometimes they hear that message and it's challenging to overcome that because that throws up an obstacle.

The noun *obstacle* shows Jerry's assessment of this situation. Jerry thinks this situation is very *challenging*. Again, we see that history does not have the same stature as other school subjects and, according to these teachers, students are getting that message. This idea is influencing students' attitudes toward history and oftentimes creating an *obstacle* for history teachers. Students, therefore, implicitly or explicitly, are exposed to the message that history is not a valuable school subject.

**Students' Limited Skills and Background**

The focus teachers emphasized some challenges related to the limited skills students bring to the history classroom. This was a particularly salient theme, due to the characteristics of teachers' school districts as low-income and highly diverse communities.

*Students' Limited Reading Skills.* In talking about reading in history, Maggie stated that "getting students to read" is a great problem in today's schools. Maggie is especially aware of the importance of reading in history classes and mentioned students' inability to access texts as a major challenge for her in teaching history. She said that "the vast majority of the students that I get are not good readers, so they don't enjoy reading." Maggie's use of the negative markers *are not good readers* and *they don't enjoy reading* reflect students' lack of these skills while at the same time pointing to the need to develop these skills, especially in history.

Jerry also recognizes the significance of reading for teaching and learning school history and finds it difficult to deal with kids who cannot read the textbook: "These kids in this area, they simply tune it out. They do not read it [the history textbook]. It's really obvious that they don't read, and to take history class in U.S. history you gotta be able to read books about history." Jerry, like Maggie, also utilizes negation, expressed in *they do not read it* and *they don't read,* to express students' limited reading skills. Here we see the juxtaposition of what students are not able to do, expressed in *they do not read it,* and what they need to do, marked by the use of *you gotta be able to read books about history.* Both Maggie and Jerry recognize that history teaching and learning is highly dependent on students being able to access text. Jo, a 5th-grade teacher, stressed the role of reading and writing in history: "History involves a great deal of reading and writing in order to interpret events and their effect on modern times." Students' limited reading skills are seen as a major challenge in teaching history, since history is largely dependent on texts.

***Students' Limited Foundation in History.*** Students' limited foundation in history refers to their lack of historical background knowledge and problems with particular historical skills coming into history courses. For instance, Maggie reported that students coming to her 11th-grade class lack historical background knowledge. Students' lack of historical background is partly due, in Maggie's view, to a focus on other requirements, such as reading and math, in previous years:

> Many of them have not had any kind of social studies at all since maybe 6th grade—we don't have a requirement in this district for 9th grade. Their knowledge of geography is just appalling. It's not uncommon for high school students to not be aware that California is not a country. I'm serious. They live in the Sacramento region and yet they can't tell you what the capital is. They do not understand the use of the word *state* in "United States" or as foreign states. I had one person a year or so ago that absolutely could not wrap her head around the fact that there was Mexico and there was New Mexico.

Here, Maggie links history to the importance of other areas of social studies. This issue is especially difficult for her due to the characteristics of her district.

Maggie explained her students' limited foundation: "I've had kids come into my class where we are supposed to start with reconstruction after the Civil War, and their response is, 'What is the Civil War?'" In Maggie's view, students' lack of historical background coupled with the number of state requirements history teachers need to cover create an especially problematic situation. For Maggie, there is a close connection between students' experience with history and their historical knowledge development. Maggie believes students are not to blame for their lack of content knowledge, and she attributes the whole problem of students' need for background knowledge in history to their lack of experience with history in previous grades. According to Maggie, because history is not a major focus in her district, students are not exposed to history as often as they should be. Maggie acknowledged that students' "foundation is very limited when they get to me, and I don't get them until they're in 11th grade. It's really, really difficult sometimes to get them to make the connection." Maggie's use of the intensifier *really* twice and the adjective *difficult* shows the relationship between students' inadequate background and the challenges she faces as a history teacher.

For Peter, instructional challenges lie in the area of teaching analysis in history. He claims that students come to his classroom with notions that they do not have to write complete sentences or whole paragraphs that require "higher order thinking skills." Getting students to analyze the information presented in history is of extreme importance for Peter. He voiced concern about some teachers requiring students to provide simple answers just because they are easier to correct. For instance, if a question is, "What was the center of the Roman Empire?" the answer is a one-word response. But if teachers ask more complex questions, they need to take the time to carefully read students' answers:

> If you were to say… "Did Franklin Roosevelt's New Deal contain elements of fascism and communism or was it pretty much middle of the road type of policies? Explain why," you can't just answer. You need to understand all those things and then explain those things to get your point across. You can't just give that to somebody else to grade. You have to read them [the student responses].

Moving students from simple answers to more complex analysis requires time and effort on the part of history teachers. In addition, Peter believes it is challenging for history teachers to give assignments that are more involved because students require immediate feedback. Middle and high school teachers typically have 150 students across five classes, so providing this "immediate" feedback is a challenge for them.

Tom finds the major difficulty in teaching history to be communicating complex ideas: "Getting kids to understand long, drawn out concepts, from the Enlightenment to the Great Awakening to trade issues, is much more difficult." For Tom, this is a major part of history learning. In addition, Tom finds it challenging to help students understand and make connections between different historical agents and their motivations to act in certain ways. Tom recognizes that some students are able to make connections and understand these concepts, but many of his students are not able to establish these types of relationships. Tom differentiated between developing historical understanding and memorizing dates, contending that some of his students are "still trying to remember 1776." Tom places value in understanding "those broad concepts and really internalizing."

Jerry considers students' lack of prior knowledge in history as the biggest challenge he has had to deal with:

> Lack of prior knowledge. The kids that do best in history are the ones that can demonstrate some prior knowledge where they've heard of the Civil

War, they've heard of the Declaration of Independence. They even might know what's in it more or less, things like that. There are some that literally have not heard of those things and you can't fault them for that. They may have come from other countries or just have backgrounds where there's no exposure to that, so when they come into it, the ones that have low prior knowledge, low levels of prior knowledge, they don't do as well because they can't connect to context quite as much. Just kind of an off the top of my head example would be, let's say that we're studying something like what I call the freedom documents like the Magna Carta,... if I can start out with something like Thomas Jefferson was instrumental in the Virginia Statute for Religious Freedom, can anybody else tell me what else he really contributed to a lot? Declaration of Independence. The kind of kids that raise their hand and they understand that Jefferson participated strongly in the Declaration will therefore understand a little bit about his point of view and they will know that he's bringing certain attitudes to the table in this new thing, whereas the kids that don't know Thomas Jefferson, it won't mean anything. It's like there's this dude named Thomas Jefferson, so what? And so that's the contrast between high prior knowledge and low prior knowledge. There's even prior knowledge within the context of one class. In other words, some kids are gonna do better at remembering that four months ago we studied the Constitution and it has these amendments and some are much more able to connect those, whereas others have completely forgotten about them, or more likely didn't learn it in the first place.

Like Maggie, Jerry considers students' lack of historical background knowledge as the major challenge in teaching history. He also does not hold students responsible overall for this issue. Jerry and Maggie blame the system and recognize that students have not had opportunities to develop their historical background knowledge. Nonetheless, it is clear that this is still a barrier. Students with limited experience with history may struggle more to connect concepts they talk about in class to other historical events. It is easier for kids to make connections when they have some historical background on certain topics and events.

***High Demands of the History Curriculum and the Teaching of Writing.*** In addition to students' limited skills and background, the content area of history as a discipline poses challenges for teaching as it relates to the teaching of school history writing. History as a content area places high demands on teachers, especially in terms of institutional pressures to develop standards-based curriculum and prepare students for standardized tests. These challenges have implications for the teaching of writing in history. The teachers are aware of these challenges and their influence on the teaching and learning of history, the focus of this section. These expectations have a clear effect on what teachers select to include in their history classes.

Maggie considers the many state requirements a major challenge for what teachers must do and cover in history. She is particularly critical of the history-social science standards: "Whoever it was that put together those standards was interested in coverage more than understanding, quite obviously because there's way too much." Her criticism of coverage being more valued than students' understanding in state requirements is mirrored by research in history teaching that claims that there is an "addiction to coverage" common in high schools, especially in history (Newman, 1988, p. 346). This issue is especially difficult for Maggie due to the characteristics of her district, where students need much background knowledge. In addition, she believes that the standards are "unrealistic":

> It's really tough because you know you can mention something and touch on it, but that doesn't mean that the kids understand what it's about and there are just so many things that they've got into in the standards that I think are of dubious value, quite honestly. They are not the most important things that I think the kids have to understand, so it's difficult for me. When you talk about the whole frontier experience and what that, the effect that that has had on the character of the American people, they need time to understand what that experience was, and they don't.

Maggie contrasts what history teachers need to do and details that are not important. This contrast is constructed through her language: *you can mention something and touch on it, but that doesn't mean that the kids understand.* The connector *but* draws a distinction between mentioning something and understanding it. Maggie also contrasts *so many things . . . in the standards that . . . are of dubious value*—things that she considers unnecessary for students to know—with other, more important and relevant historical issues that students need time to understand. Some standards are not what she values as a history teacher. Students certainly need enough time to really understand historical concepts and develop historical understanding; just "mentioning" or "touching on" certain issues is not enough. Maggie's use of the adjectives *tough* and *difficult* to describe history teaching shows her assessment of the situation and the challenges with which she has had to deal. Maggie sees the issue of time as an extremely important component of history teaching so that she can teach and assess depth instead of just coverage and simple memorization of information.

Peter also discussed the high demands of the history curriculum, focusing primarily on how they affect history teachers' teaching of school history writing. Peter finds that many history teachers do not believe they are responsible for addressing writing in the history classroom and often find they either lack adequate resources to address writing or just do not have enough time to focus on writing because of the many demands placed on them by state requirements and standards and the realities of the classroom.

State requirements and standards also have a clear effect on Tom's classroom, especially in regard to the writing assignments that he requires. In answering a question about assigning research papers in his classes, Tom noted, "I don't have enough of any one thing or of any general topic to really spend a lot of time doing research with, and plus we are so pressed to do standards-based education that a lot of times we just don't get to the research part." Like Maggie, Tom feels that not enough time can be spent on any one topic because of the many state requirements and standards that history teachers must cover. He frames this as a challenge to develop longer projects with his students and wishes he had more time to spend on extended assignments. Tom sees that history teachers are *pressed* to use standards. His use of this word implies an outside force that clearly affects his teaching. This outside force may prevent him from doing certain tasks that he might do if this particular influence were not present. Tom, in talking about his own challenge in teaching, said,

> I probably don't use it [writing] enough, or I fall off somewhere along the year doing it. It's a lot of the problem I have is staying consistent through the year about what I'm doing. A lot of times I start strong then start dropping off. When things get tense and tight, I don't get enough written.

This may be quite common for teachers at the early stages in their career. Tom's use of *when things get tense and tight* indicates that the high demands of the history curriculum clearly affect his teaching and, consequently, the learning opportunities of his students. In addition, Tom's use of the word *pressed* in the previous extract is closely related to *tense and tight*, showing both external and internal influences in his teaching. The use of these words suggests challenges that have affected Tom's teaching.

Jerry, like Peter and Tom, describes a challenge for teaching writing in school history. In terms of teaching school history writing in particular, Jerry finds it very challenging to grade students' writing on a regular basis. Having to teach approximately 150 students, he assigns writing but has found an alternative to looking at every student's assignments every week:

> Because I think what happens is that when you have as many kids as I have— I've got 150 kids, it hovers between 150, 160—there's no way I can read all of them [their assignments]. It just wouldn't work. If I had 80 kids, I could

probably do it, but just sort of given the school system and the practicalities of it, there's a way in which I kind of have to say I'm gonna look through this stack of homework and I'm gonna read some of them thoroughly and look at a few of them kind of cursorily and hope that a lot of that averages, will mean that I look at one kid's paper at some point during the year. It's unfortunate, but that's the reality of modern day public school teaching.

From this example of Jerry's experience, it is clear that he finds it challenging to attend to his students' writing because of what he faces at school. In this extract, Jerry juxtaposes his wishes and the challenges he faces as a history teacher. This juxtaposition is found throughout this extract. For instance, Jerry juxtaposes what he wishes he had through the use of the conditional clause *If I had 80 kids*, and the reality of the school system, *I've got 150 kids*. Jerry discusses how *there's no way* he can read all of his students' writing assignments and *there's a way* that he found to solve this problem. Because of these realities, Jerry considers it difficult to address writing issues in the classroom, saying, "Sometimes there isn't time to do that" due to the many demands of the school history curriculum. Jerry thinks this situation is *unfortunate*, which indicates his judgment of this condition.

***Impact of Challenges on the Teaching of Writing.*** This section demonstrates the importance of challenges in the instructional decisions teachers make. All four focus teachers reported how the challenges affected how much they could focus on writing in history. They stressed the importance of reading, writing, and analysis in school history but found it particularly challenging to focus on these skills effectively because of many curricular constraints, lack of time, and students' limited abilities. A significant finding is that students' limited foundation in history was considered a special challenge that teachers have to deal with and a major hurdle for the teaching and learning of history, especially taking into account the priority given to reading and math in state requirements. Since history teaching is not emphasized much in school, the implicit and explicit message that both history teachers and students are getting is that "history doesn't count" (see de Oliveira, 2008).

The focus teachers raised instructional issues that were related to the teaching of reading, writing, and analysis and wished for fewer standards to cover so that more time could be spent on the development of these skills. Teachers indicated that there is not enough time to fully develop students' historical understanding due not only to the many standards and state requirements, but also to students' lack of content knowledge of history, in part attributable to their limited exposure to history in previous schooling experiences. In addition, students' difficulties with reading were cast as part of the explanation for their limited experience, background information, and understanding of history, all of which contribute to the challenge of having to spend more time covering concepts that students need in order to understand subsequent concepts and periods.

Despite these challenges, these focus history teachers see that writing may be able to support attainment of goals for history. In the following section, drawing on questionnaire data from 44 history teachers, I describe reported perspectives of a larger group of teachers about the role of writing in history and their instructional practices with regard to writing.

## Teachers' Perspectives and Instructional Practices in Teaching Writing

In order to understand teachers' views on the significance of writing in history, history teachers were asked to consider what role writing has in history classes. In addition, teachers also reported how they use and teach writing in their classes.

### *Teachers' Perspectives on Writing*

Teachers were asked to state what they thought the role of writing was in history. Analyses indicated that teachers' responses emphasized writing as representing two interconnected functions: Writing to *display* understanding and writing to *develop* understanding. All teachers in this study found writing to have an important role in history classes. Several teachers described the role of writing as *critical, important, essential,* and *a must.*

#### Writing to Display Understanding

Many of the participating teachers think of writing in history as an essential way for students to demonstrate their knowledge of the content area. As one teacher put it, "Writing is a way to express what the students have learned over a course of study" (Robert, 8th-grade teacher). Another teacher explained, "Students need to learn to express themselves formally and be able to support their opinions in a coherent and logical manner" (Bianca, 11th-grade teacher). An 8th-grade teacher, Connor, summarizes this function well:

> The students must organize their thoughts and demonstrate through the writing process just what they know about any given historical event or person. How else can they show what they are thinking, as an individual, about a subject if they do not write? No multiple choice test can really assess a student's knowledge like writing an essay at the end of an instructional unit.

One half of the responses focused on this function of writing as display of understanding.

### Writing to Develop Understanding

Several teachers conceptualized writing as an essential tool for students to develop their understanding of history. One teacher said that "writing helps students understand the history" (Jo, 5th-grade teacher). Writing serves the function of helping students to develop subject matter understanding since as they write they are deepening their knowledge of history. Writing "allows for development of ideas" (Ruben, 11th-grade teacher). Responses emphasized that as students write, they develop more knowledge about history. Another teacher identified essential skills students develop as they write: "They have to be able to persuade, explain, defend a point of view. They have to be able to summarize what took place. They have to be able to put their opinion into words" (Kelly, 8th-grade teacher). Lori, a 7th-grade teacher, reported that writing "is a great way for students to process the information they have taken in and do some analyzing and synthesizing and work on articulation."

Writing is seen by teachers as important for success in high school, college, and life. According to teachers' responses, students need as much practice as possible as they learn to communicate not only orally, but in written form. Writing is considered essential to the study of history, specifically for building critical thinking and analysis skills. One teacher emphasized the importance of writing even when students are required to develop a visual project: "[E]ven when I assign a visual project, they have a written component included" (Kerry, 10th-grade teacher). Another teacher emphasized the importance of writing as it is connected to the nature of history as a subject: "Students need to write about history in order to make it more than a list of facts." Writing "helps students focus on their thought processes and gives a reference point from which they can learn" (Gabriel, 10th- and 11th-grade teacher).

Writing is used in history classes as a form of display of students' understanding and knowledge of historical events. Writing is also considered by some teachers as a way to develop students' understanding of the subject matter. Students write not only to demonstrate what they know but also to discover what their understanding is. This dual function of writing in history emphasizes the need for better and consistent writing instruction in history classes, which is what I turn to in the next section. While this section focused on teachers' perspectives about the role of writing in school history, the following section identifies some instructional practices of history teachers in regard to writing instruction.

## *Teachers' Instructional Practices*

Teachers spoke of "teaching writing" in several ways and included several different conceptions of what it means to teach writing in history. For many of the teachers, teaching writing means explaining what the requirements are to students, including essay structure, criteria for writing assignments, and expectations for short answer questions. For others, teaching writing means going over structural issues with students. For example, they spoke of explaining essay components (*introduction, body,* and *conclusion*). Still others conceptualized teaching writing as involving stages and strategies ("teaching writing as a process"). The "writing stages" were conceptualized as either prewriting–writing–editing or topic sentence writing–paragraph writing–essay writing.

When teachers were asked whether they provided writing instruction in their history classes, 32 teachers responded positively, while 12 teachers said they do not teach writing in their history classes (results on these teachers are presented later in this chapter). Here, I report on the answers of teachers who responded that they provide some kind of instruction in writing. The analysis revealed four distinct categories associated with the level of attention given to writing and writing instruction in school history. Teachers' statements were placed in each of the categories according to their reported ways of dealing with writing in history. The first category means that teachers provided minimal writing instruction in their teaching. The second category includes some attention and instruction in writing. The third category demonstrates cases where there is some more active instructional scaffolding of writing. The final category indicates deep scaffolding of writing and active attention to writing instruction.

### Minimal Attention to Writing

Teachers described ways in which they use writing in history with minimal attention to writing instruction. For instance, some teachers spoke of explaining to students what they require in terms of writing, but they do not systematically provide writing instruction. Statements under this category conceptualized their writing instruction as using writing to assess students rather than as an active focus on instructing students in elements of writing. From the 32 history teachers who said that they teach writing in their classes, five fall under this category.

George, an 11th-grade teacher in a low-income, diverse district, spoke of the inclusion of a unit on study skills in his teaching, which included textbook assessment, notetaking, and paragraph and essay writing. Catherine, a 10th-grade teacher, reported how her school has been "developing rubrics which make it easier for students to analyze and understand the various criteria of the writing assignments as well as for teachers to evaluate the writing that our students produce." Constance, a 10th- and 11th-grade teacher, said that she reviews "how to . . . seek answers and solutions with the resources available: how to 'de-code' information, to make educated decisions on the information researched." These can be considered as minimal writing instruction. In general, teachers provided students with the writing requirements or explained what they expected from student writing.

### Some Attention to Writing

Teachers spoke of ways in which they provide some attention to writing and some writing instruction. When teachers talked about explaining the basics of essay writing (such as *introduction, body,* and *conclusion*) and using strategies such as summary writing, they were included in this category. This is the largest category, with 10 teachers falling under it. Harry, an 8th-grade teacher, reported that he demonstrates "all that I require my students to do. I share my current writing and my first paper from college. . . . I explain the basics of Introduction, Body, and Conclusion on a regular basis." A 10th- and 11th-grade teacher, Kerry, mentioned that he teaches students "how to write a basic five paragraph essay at the beginning of the first semester." However, it was unclear whether Kerry scaffolds that process with any degree of detail.

### Active Scaffolding of Writing Instruction

Some teachers reported ways in which they actively scaffold writing instruction in their history classes. These teachers mentioned different skills and strategies that they use with their students throughout the year. Teachers under this category provide instruction in elements of writing. Jean, a 10th- and 11th-grade teacher, reported that she teaches "the students every year basic organizational skills for writing . . . thesis statements, paragraph construction, formula essay writing." Jeff, an 8th-grade teacher, usually teaches students "how to include questions in answers, give more details, and have good intro and concluding paragraphs." Seven teachers were included in this category.

### Deep Scaffolding of Writing Instruction

Some teachers described ways in which they provided writing instruction and provided a deep scaffolding of writing for students. These teachers mentioned not only different skills and strategies that they have used with their students throughout the year but also how they explicitly explained what the requirements for writing assignments are. For example, one 8th-grade teacher, Julie, spoke of how she teaches and reinforces the "writing process" in her classroom and includes 11-sentence paragraphs and uses them to get students to gather evidence and place it in a logical order in the paragraphs. This category includes six teachers.

Some teachers reported that they do not teach writing in history. Eight teachers said that they do not provide writing instruction, while four teachers reported that they do not focus on writing in history because their students already receive instruction in writing from them in their Language Arts classes. These four teachers are responsible for teaching "core," a combination of Language Arts and History classes with specific periods dedicated to each. The eight teachers who reported that they do not provide writing instruction in history indicated that they rely on the Language Arts teachers for instruction in writing but often use rubrics and prompts to assess students in history.

One salient result from the responses was that there was no consistent manner in which teachers from a certain grade level addressed writing. Responses differed in the amount of instruction provided and in the type of instruction provided. Furthermore, most of the teachers emphasized structural and organizational issues. Answers varied from structural issues ("explain introduction, body, and conclusion") to inclusion of strategies, with many teachers emphasizing the process approach to writing.

This section pointed out some relevant issues related to the challenges teachers face in history and issues related to writing instruction. Teachers' perspectives about the role of writing emphasize a dual function of writing in history, highlighting the need for better and consistent writing instruction in history classes. Students write not only to demonstrate what they know but also to develop and discover their understanding. This dual function of writing in history emphasizes the need for better and consistent writing instruction in history classes, considering the challenges that history teachers who work in highly diverse neighborhoods face and how these challenges affect the teaching of writing in history.

## Discussion and Implications

This chapter has presented the unique challenges that history teachers face when teaching history and addressing writing in low-income, diverse schools in California and the teachers' reported practices using and teaching writing in school history. The analysis drew on questionnaire data from 44 history teachers and interview data from 4 focus teachers with different levels of teaching experience. The four focus teachers perceived similar challenges at the societal, institutional, and classroom levels. The findings reveal that these challenges were conceptualized as multi-dimensional, complex, and interconnected issues. All of the challenges had an effect in these teachers' classrooms. Because of this, it is fair to conclude that students' learning of history is influenced by how these challenges affect the teachers' instruction of history.

The questionnaire teachers spoke of teaching writing in several ways and communicated several different conceptions of what it means to provide writing instruction in history. These conceptions include explaining what the requirements are to students, such as essay structure guidelines, criteria for writing assignments, and expectations for short answer questions; going over structural issues with students, such as explaining essay components; and teaching students writing strategies. The analysis revealed four distinct categories associated with the level of attention given to writing and writing instruction in school history. Teachers did not provide a consistent way of addressing writing at each grade level. Responses differed in terms of the amount of instruction provided and the type of instruction provided. Furthermore, most of the teachers emphasized structural and organizational issues without a clear understanding of how to raise students' awareness about the linguistic features that make up different genres of history.

This chapter has illustrated teachers' views of the importance of writing in history. As the chapter has stressed, writing instruction is often minimal in history classes, providing little scaffolding for history learners, particularly given the current lack of adequate teaching of history, limited student prior knowledge of historical events and themes, and the demanding nature of historical writing.

The goals that teachers hold for history as a school subject, discussed in the first section of this chapter, include stressing the importance of teachers' work on historical sequencing and providing students with knowledge about history, getting students excited about history, and helping students learn that history is about interpretation. These goals cannot be met through simple coverage of factual information in curriculum and cannot be assessed through multiple-choice testing. Writing can support these goals in several ways, as will be discussed in Chapter Seven.

Teacher responses overwhelmingly emphasized the importance of writing in history. However, a discrepancy can be seen when we consider teachers' perspectives on the role of writing in history and their emphasis on writing instruction. While teachers see writing as an important aspect of history, there are a number of other factors that influence teachers' decisions about what to teach in history. The challenges that the focus teachers discussed clearly affect their writing instruction in history. Even the small number of teachers who provide deep scaffolding of writing would benefit from a better understanding of the role of language in students' demonstration of their historical understanding. Most teachers focused on aspects of organization and structure but did not seem to see how linguistic features contribute to the organization and structure of writing. This is not surprising, given the fact that history teachers do not typically receive any kind of professional development in explicit ways to deal with language in their subject area.

These findings indicate that it would be beneficial for teachers to develop a better understanding of the role of language in history learning. They also point to the need for teacher education and professional development programs to assist teachers with ways to better incorporate writing instruction in history. Teachers can expand their knowledge of the significance of writing in history classes. As this chapter highlighted, writing is widely used as an assessment instrument for students and as a way for students to develop historical understanding.

Eskey's (1993) words that opened this chapter provide the background for some concluding ideas presented here. History holds the potential to improve students' literacy while developing their historical understanding, since reading and writing are an integral part of history teaching and learning. History can provide a motivating environment where students can develop as readers and writers. This content area can serve as a medium for improving students' reading and writing in general because students can develop knowledge about disciplinary expectations—how writing for history may be different from writing in other school subjects.

The insights gained from the history teachers in this study can help teacher educators recognize the range of ways that writing is addressed in school history. They can also help professional development providers plan for workshops and presentations that focus on writing development across grade levels.

# 4

## *Student Writing in History*

### *8th Grade*

The next two chapters focus on texts, the texts written by 8th- and 11th-grade students and teachers' expectations for those texts. What are the expectations for students' expository writing at the 8th-grade level in school history? What are the language features that enable students to write an expository genre in school history? How can we help students move from where they are to where they should be? I start out with a discussion and analysis of the two 8th-grade teachers' expectations for the expository writing task. The next section presents two essays that were considered successful by the teacher. First, in presenting the analysis of Text One, the linguistic constructs and language resources that will be the focus of the analyses of all of the essays in the chapter are described in detail. Following Text One, I use another example of a successful essay in order to show how certain language resources construe a highly valued text, particularly in terms of its organization and overall structure. The focus is then on English Language Learners' (ELLs') writing. I present two examples of the writing of mainstreamed ELLs to illustrate the language choices that these students make and suggest resources that still need to be developed. Text Three is an example of an ELL essay that needs improvement on both content and

*Knowing and Writing School History,* pages 49–88
Copyright © 2011 by Information Age Publishing
All rights of reproduction in any form reserved.

organization of writing, and Text Four exemplifies a successful essay. The analyses of these four essays take note of some language features that are functional for performing this task and that could be the focus of pedagogy in history classrooms. The texts illustrate some key linguistic features used by 8th-grade students in response to a prompt that elicited the exposition genre. I use the term *exposition,* following Martin's (2002) description of the genres of history, to refer to what History Project (HP) leaders and teachers call an *argument. Exposition* is a genre in which a particular interpretation is presented in a thesis that needs justification in the form of historical information (Martin, 2002). This term is closely related to what the HP prompt elicited from students.

These texts are representative of the corpus of 24 8th-grade essays analyzed. As described in Chapter One, these essays were collected as part of an evaluation study that investigated the professional development work done by the HP.

The analyses are based on a functional linguistic framework, which sees language not as a set of rules to be followed, but rather as a set of language choices for making meaning (Halliday & Matthiessen, 2004). Language varies because what we do with language varies. The analyses presented focus on the lexical and grammatical resources that 8th-grade students draw on to write an exposition, and the analyses illustrate the significance of the point of departure of each clause, the importance of effective logical connections, and the importance of elaborating and reiterating ideas.

## Teachers' Expectations for the Expository Writing Task

In this section, I draw on the discourse-based interviews to describe what teachers expected of students with each essay task at the 8th-grade level. The two 8th-grade focus teachers, Tom and Jerry, were asked to express their expectations for the specific writing prompt and to select essays that they considered in need of improvement on both content and process of writing and essays they evaluated as strong on both the content and process of writing. These history teachers are experts in their content area and know their students' skills best, so they are the most appropriate authorities to assess their students' school history writing. Examples of more successful and less successful essays are presented to illustrate the differences found in essays that teachers rated differently.

The expository writing task was used in 8th-grade history classes as part of the evaluation study. The students were responding to a prompt that asked whether the framers of the Constitution were successful in achieving a balance of power or whether one branch had more powers than the other two. The prompt presented these two positions as questions. The prompt was an extended one that included the following parts: (1) some background on the creation of a new form of government detailed in a new Constitution, the organization of government into three branches (legislative, executive, and judicial), and why the "checks and balances" were designed; (2) a specific question that students were supposed to address; and (3) specific rhetorical features that students were expected to include (i.e., thesis, evidence, analysis, conclusion). Students were also expected to discuss at least two reasons for their answer by providing specific examples from the Constitution to support their thesis. Some students chose to respond that the balance of power was achieved, while others said that one branch was more powerful. These different views were reflected in what the teachers said. In the interviews, each 8th-grade teacher was asked a series of questions following the structure of the prompt so that they could express their expectations about what the essays should include.

The 8th-grade teachers did not agree on the best answer to the question. Jerry expected students to respond that the framers of the Constitution were successful in achieving a balance of power. According to Jerry, this is demonstrated in part by the fact that the system is still with us today. Jerry mentioned that students could use several examples as support for this position. For instance, students could talk about the president's vetoing power over legislation that he or she does not support. Another example would be the Supreme Court's power to decide on the constitutionality of laws, therefore checking the Legislature. Students could also cite an example in history where that happened, namely, in the case of *Marbury v. Madison*, profiled in the textbook used in the district (Stuckey & Salvucci, 2003). This was the U.S. Supreme Court case that established the principle of judicial review. According to Jerry, this case can exemplify that there are precedents in history for showing that the system has worked and can work. Students could be more general or more specific in their answers, either providing some general information on each of the branch's powers and how the system is supposed to work or providing specific historical information about historical cases when the balance of power could be seen.

Teachers also had expectations for the structuring of the essay. Jerry expected to see the thesis being presented in the first paragraph of the essay, with the writer's position on the question clearly stated to answer the question posed in the prompt. Jerry mentioned that 8th graders typically have difficulty addressing the question. Often students have strong ideas but do not develop them in the essay by providing historical information to support them. One of the main problems students have, according to Jerry, is that they write in a "speaking style" not appropriate for academic writing.

Jerry also expected that students would conclude the essay "by bringing it back" to the main point or thesis.

Tom, on the other hand, suggested that students could take the position that one branch was more powerful than the others. He mentioned, for example, that a possible interpretation is that the framers of the Constitution were deliberately making the legislative branch the strongest. According to Tom, they did not expect the judicial review to expand the way it did. In addition, they did not expect the president to be chosen more by the people after the Electoral College was established, which somewhat democratized the system. Tom stated that this increased the power of the executive branch. Tom also mentioned *Marbury v. Madison*, which increased the judicial power. These historical events set the precedent for the two branches to gain power. In addition, students could also go through other examples throughout history and discuss the shifts in power, such as when a popular president like Jackson would increase the power of the president while an unpopular one like Hoover would decrease it. However, these expectations would be for students who have a strong background in history. Tom recognizes that his students are just starting to learn U.S. history. In elementary school, they are exposed to just a few topics, and Tom does not expect students to come to him already knowing how to analyze history. After Tom looked at students' essays in more detail, he said the following about the students' answers in general:

> These answers are acceptable since they [the students] come to me almost like *tabula rasa* in terms of U.S. history and government, and showing that they can learn how it works and what the pieces are, that demonstrates some knowing and understanding. Right now I want to put the pieces together and the foundation so that they understand how the structure works, how everything functions. They're going to get more of this in the 11th grade and even more in 12th grade, so I'm not too worried about government structures and how they work. As long as they understand that the president doesn't make laws, and it's a whole bunch of other people that are elected and the president is just supposed to enforce it, and they see some antagonism between them and they know that the Supreme Court theoretically holds this structure or this power next to them, then I'm very happy because now they have a working foundation they can work on. When they go to 11th grade, they can take that with them and build more detail and finesse to it, more politics that play in the government.

Tom's words show what he expects students to know at the 8th-grade level and what he finds important in terms of historical concepts that can serve as "foundation" for students to take on in later grades.

Some important points have to be highlighted about Jerry's and Tom's discussion of their expectations for this writing task. Jerry, on the one hand, not only talked about the content of students' answers, but also mentioned how the content was to be expressed (e.g., a position in a thesis presented in the introduction, provision of historical information to support the position, and a conclusion that brings the whole essay back to the main point or thesis). Tom, on the other hand, focused his answers on the content itself, stressing what the ideal answer would be in comparison to what he anticipated students' answers to include. Tom recognized that when reading these essays, one cannot forget where the students are coming from, that is, their lack of familiarity with U.S. history. These differences were also reflected in how they looked at and assessed students' essays, as I will demonstrate in the analysis.

## Text Analysis and Results

I now present two essays considered successful. First, I describe the language resources that are the focus of the essay analyses presented in the chapter, explaining the linguistic constructs by looking at the essays in detail.

The texts used in this chapter to illustrate some key lexical and grammatical features employed by 8th-grade students are representative of the corpus of 24 8th-grade essays analyzed. The essays illustrate the language resources that these students bring to this task and suggest resources that they still need to develop. The linguistic features are those that are functional for accomplishing the goals of the expository writing task.

Particular texts exemplify only certain features of the range of language resources that may be employed when students write an expository essay. Other examples would bring other resources into focus. However, the texts presented here are representative of the variety and range of resources used by students. Another important consideration is that these texts are first drafts written under time pressure. Students did not have time to improve their drafts. As Jerry put it, "We have to account for the fact that we're timing it. This is coming out of their memory, so it creates a different kind of essay than it would otherwise."

It is also important to consider the characteristics of the students whose texts are presented. Students from District 1 are racially and ethnically diverse. Most of the district's students are disadvantaged, with 68% of the students eligible for free/reduced lunch. Approximately 25% of the district's students are ELLs. These students present many difficult socio-economic challenges. Even the writers whose essays were considered effective are not strong writers. The essays are not examples of sophisticated writing and they need improvement in the areas of historical information and claims. Yet differences between the writers can be shown by the analysis. The texts presented have been assessed as successful essays. The following analyses shows key linguistic features that 8th-grade students are drawing on when they write and that enable them to meet the expectations of the task and their teacher. The functional linguistic constructs used in the chapter are identified in the context of the analysis of Text One and then taken up again in the remaining texts.

All of the essays from the corpus had historical inaccuracies. Teachers tolerated these inaccuracies, particularly knowing that students come to the 8th grade not having received a lot of instruction in U.S. history. For example, in one of the essays that will be analyzed, the writer confuses the executive and legislative branches and describes the executive branch as *in charge of* the House of Representatives and the Senate. In another essay, the last part of the statement *Like for a bill to become a law it must first pass through the houses of Congress then go through the other branches* is incorrect. After a bill passes through the houses of Congress, it goes to the president's desk for the signature or the veto. In another essay, the student writes, *And I think it's the executive branch because that's the branch that controls the army and the president.* The teacher who assessed this essay reported that the student should have said that "the president is the head of the executive branch and therefore the commander in chief of the army." Several other examples of historical inaccuracies were identified by the two teachers.

Texts One and Two are examples of successful essays. The analysis of Text One shows how the writer has used lexical and grammatical resources to construct an essay that was considered effective. In discussing Text One, I present how the information was organized and developed throughout the essay and highlight the language choices that realize the good organization.

## Text One

The writer of Text One starts out this essay by answering the question posed in the prompt, which asked whether the framers of the Constitution were successful in achieving a balance of power between the three branches of power. Then paragraphs two, three, and four define and explain each branch. The position statement *I guess so* shows that the writer did not have a strong sense of exactly what he was going to present. However, after this introductory clause, the writer's position becomes clearer, with the thesis *because if the government had not been split into 3 branches, they would have too much power causing people to get angry.* The conclusion comes back to the point of power and control, ending with a comment about the importance

---

**TEXT ONE**

I guess so, because if the government had not been split into 3 branches, they would have too much power causing people to get angry. To keep the power balanced they needed to split the powers. They made sure each branch had an equal amount of power through checks and balances.

The executive branch is in charge of the House of Representatives and the Senate. They decide what laws to make, but it must be approved by the president.

The legislative branch deals with the law. If any new rule is passed, it must be followed.

The judicial branch contains the Supreme Court and [it] takes care of any thing relating to problems with crime, murder, etc.

If the government was not divided into three branches, the government would have too much power and control over people. It may result to chaos to everyone. It is also a good thing the government is divided because they can get pretty stupid and with the power almost do any thing they want, especially presidents.

---

of the division of the government. This last comment is a critical position regarding the government's actions and shows the writer's development of an analytical perspective. Even though the writer confuses the historical points made about two of the branches, the teacher considered this essay effective compared to other essays in the set. The linguistic features that this writer used are highlighted below. These include thematic choices that help the writer to structure information, logical connectors that enable the presentation of logical meanings, cohesive resources that refer back to points already made, and elaboration of major ideas. Each one of these is described in the context of the analysis of Text One.

### Theme and Method of Development

A functional linguistic construct valuable for understanding the presentation of information in a text is *theme/rheme progression*. *Theme* in English is the element that comes first in a clause (Halliday & Matthiessen, 2004). Theme is "the point of departure of the message" (Halliday, 1994, p. 37). The remainder of the message is the *rheme*. For example, in the clause "The legislative branch deals with the law," *The legislative branch* is the theme and *deals with the law* is the rheme.

Analysis of the organization of information in this text serves as a means of understanding the method of development of the text. The point of departure or *theme* of each clause is significant in two ways. First, the beginning of the English clause is fundamental because it shows the writer's point of departure for the clause and relates it to the rest of the text (Halliday, 1994). Second, themes function as cohesive elements within a text and play a major role in the organization of a text as a message.

Table 4.1 presents the thematic analysis of Text One, with themes in bold face. Marked themes are indicated by an asterisk at the end of the theme. Shaded lines indicate change in paragraphs.

The thematic structure gives the clause its character as a message (Halliday, 1994). For analytical purposes, the theme is considered to continue up to and include the first ideational element, which is a participant, circumstance, or process. This ideational constituent is referred to as *the topical theme* (Halliday & Matthiessen, 2004). In English declarative clauses, the theme typically coincides with the subject of the clause. Halliday (1994) refers to the realization of theme as subject as an *unmarked theme*. In clause 9, "The legislative branch deals with the law," *The legislative branch* is an unmarked theme because it is also the subject of the clause. The subject is the constituent that is chosen as theme "unless there is a good reason for choosing something else" (Halliday, 1994, p. 43). Themes that are not subject constitute *marked themes* and include circumstantial elements, such as places or times, or participants that are not the clause subject (Martin & Rose, 2003). For instance, *with the power* in clause 19 is a marked theme preceded by a textual theme *and*.

A pattern of themes, then, constructs a text's method of development. Fries (1983) defines the method of development of a text:

> (a) the lexical material placed initially within each sentence of a paragraph (i.e. the themes of each sentence of a paragraph) indicates the point of departure of the message expressed by that sentence, and (b) the information contained within the themes of all of the clauses of a paragraph creates the method of development of that paragraph. (p. 135)

Different kinds of elements can make up the theme in English. These indicate different approaches to the organization of a text. The theme can include meanings of three types: interpersonal, textual, and topical (Halliday & Matthiessen, 2004). A textual theme is a structural element such as a conjunction or a conjunctive adjunct (e.g., *and, because, therefore, as a result*). Textual themes show the relationship of a clause to the preceding text. An interpersonal theme can be a vocative, a modal, or an adjunct that expresses the writer's judgment or stance regarding the content of the message (Halliday & Matthiessen, 2004). Whole clauses can also be interpersonal

**TABLE 4.1 Thematic Analysis of Text One**

| Clause # | Theme | | | Rheme |
|---|---|---|---|---|
| | Interpersonal | Textual | Topical | |
| 1. | I guess so | because if | the government | had not been split into 3 branches, |
| 2. | | | they | would have too much power |
| 3. | | | | causing people to get angry. |
| 4. | | | To keep the power balanced* | they needed to split the powers. |
| 5. | | | They | made sure each branch had an equal amount of power through checks and balances. |
| 6. | | | The executive branch | is in charge of the House of Representatives and the Senate. |
| 7. | | | They | decide what laws to make, |
| 8. | | but | it | must be approved by the president. |
| 9. | | | The legislative branch | deals with the law. |
| 10. | | If | any new rule | is passed, |
| 11. | | | it | must be followed. |
| 12. | | | The judicial branch | contains the Supreme Court |
| 13. | | and | [The judicial branch] | takes care of any thing relating to problems with crime, murder, etc. |
| 14. | | If | the government | was not divided into three branches, |
| 15. | | | the government | would have too much power and control over people. |
| 16. | | | It | may result to chaos to everyone. |
| 17. | It is also a good thing | | the government | is divided |
| 18. | | because | they | can get pretty stupid |
| 19. | | and | with the power* | almost do any thing they want, especially presidents. |

themes, such as *It is also a good thing* in clause 17. This interpersonal theme presents the writer's perspective on the message. These are important distinctions. The writer of Text One has used a variety of themes, including unmarked themes, such as *They, The executive branch, it, The legislative branch, The judicial branch,* and *the government.* Topical themes present the first ideational element, which can be a circumstance, process, or participant.

Two common patterns of thematic progression in English are observed in these texts. The first pattern, *constant theme,* keeps the theme constant while providing new information in the rheme. The second pattern is *rheme to theme,* where the theme of a clause picks up the rheme of a previous clause. Theme typically introduces information that is presented as known or given, while new information is introduced in the rheme. A *rheme to theme movement* enables a writer to introduce new information in a clause rheme and then use it again in a subsequent clause theme, presenting it as given. Examples of these two patterns are presented in this chapter. Figure 4.1 exemplifies the two patterns.

Paragraph one starts out with an interpersonal theme, *I guess so,* that does not help the writer present a strong perspective. An assertion that responds either positively or negatively to the essay question would make the writer's position stronger. Paragraphs two, three, and four each begin with one branch as the theme of the first clause, *The executive branch* (clause 6), *The legislative branch* (clause 9), *The judicial branch* (clause 12), picking up on *the three branches* in the rheme in paragraph one. These themes function as the point of departure for the definitions and explanations about each branch, which occur in rheme position. Placing each branch in theme position is functional for defining and explaining each branch's power. This thematic construction helps the writer organize the text in predictable ways and is functional for the presentation of information. The most common

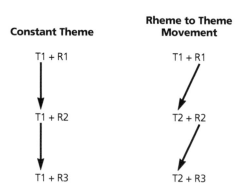

**Figure 4.1**   Constant theme and rheme to theme movement.

theme in Text One is *the government*, which enables the presentation of the information that is in rheme position in several clauses in the essay: *because if the government had not been split into 3 branches* (clause 2); *If the government was not divided into three branches, the government would have too much power and control over people* (clauses 14 and 15); and *It is also a good thing the government is divided.* The thematic choice *the government* is held constant in clauses in the introduction and the conclusion, helping the writer to move the development of ideas forward in rheme position. The focus of the information is the *split* or *division* of the government, information that is presented in the rheme.

While each clause has its thematic structure, each paragraph and essay also has a thematic structure as a whole (Martin, 1992). For Text One, the most important thematic structure is the one at the essay level. A macro-theme is the theme of the essay, or what is known in school rhetoric as a *thesis statement.* It has a predictive function as to what will be developed in the essay. In Text One, the macro-theme is *if the government had not been split into 3 branches, they would have too much power causing people to get angry.* This macro-theme is further developed in the essay, with each of the immediately following paragraphs defining and explaining the powers of the branches in turn. Macro-themes were a distinguishing feature of the more successful essays. As previously stated, the expectation for the macro-theme (thesis) was that it explicitly addressed the question posed in the prompt by providing a position that the writer would then defend in the rest of the essay.

Table 4.2 shows constant themes and rheme to theme movement. Double-sided arrows indicate rheme to theme movement. One-sided and straight arrows show constant themes.

### Elaboration

Elaboration is an especially significant linguistic construct present in many of the essays and a distinguishing characteristic that the four focus teachers highlighted. Elaboration is a type of expanding relationship whereby one clause elaborates on the meaning of another clause by restating something already presented by including additional details, clarification of points already discussed, explanation, examples, or further description (Halliday & Matthiessen, 2004; Martin & Rose, 2003). This linguistic pattern enables the rewording of statements, occurring at the level of meaning (Martin & Rose, 2003). In particular, elaboration of the macro-theme or thesis of the essay was a valued and distinguishing feature of the more successful essays.

---

## TABLE 4.2 Constant Theme, Rheme to Theme Movement: Text One

| Clause # | Topical Theme | Rheme |
|---|---|---|
| 1. | the government | had not been split into 3 branches, |
| 2. | they | would have too much power |
| 3. | | causing people to get angry. |
| 4. | To keep the power balanced | they needed to split the powers. |
| 5. | They | made sure each branch had an equal amount of power through checks and balances. |
| 6. | The executive branch | is in charge of the House of Representatives and the Senate. |
| 7. | They | decide what laws to make, |
| 8. | it | must be approved by the president. |
| 9. | The legislative branch | deals with the law. |
| 10. | any new rule | is passed, |
| 11. | it | must be followed. |
| 12. | The judicial branch | contains the Supreme Court |
| 13. | [The judicial branch] | takes care of any thing relating to problems with crime, murder, etc. |
| 14. | the government | was not divided into three branches, |
| 15. | the government | would have too much power and control over people. |
| 16. | It | may result to chaos to everyone. |
| 17. | the government | is divided |
| 18. | they | can get pretty stupid |
| 19. | with the power | almost do any thing they want, especially presidents. |

---

For instance, in Text One, the writer is using the resources of the grammar to reinforce the meanings presented in the macro-theme. The semantic notions presented in the thesis—*split into 3 branches, too much power,* and *causing people to get angry*—are taken up and elaborated in clauses 4 and 5 and clauses 14 and 15, as demonstrated in Table 4.3. Clauses 4 and 5 and 14 and 15 have a similar structure: a conditional *if* clause + result clause. Clauses 14 and 15 reinforce the message presented in the macro-theme. In addition, the meaning of the verb *causing* from clause 3 is picked up by the causal verb *result* in clause 16. Similarly, the adjective *angry* is repackaged as *chaos* while *people* is presented as *everyone*. This process of elaboration in clause 16 is achieved through the use of *grammatical metaphor,* a construct of systemic–functional linguistics that refers to making the same "meaning" with different "wording" (Halliday, 1994; Schleppegrell, 2005). Grammatical metaphor is a feature present in academic writing (Colombi, 2002; Schleppegrell, 2004, 2005).

Grammatical metaphor refers to the "transference of meaning from one kind of element to another kind" (Martin & Rose, 2003, p. 104). Halliday (Halliday & Martin, 1993) defines grammatical metaphor as

> a substitution of one grammatical structure, by another; for example *his departure* instead of *he departed.* Here the words (lexical items) are the same; what has changed is their place in the grammar. Instead of pronoun *he* + verb *departed,* functioning as Actor plus Process in a clause, we have determiner *his* + noun *departure,* functioning as a Deitic plus Thing in a nominal group. (p. 79)

When grammar and semantics correspond, participants are realized as nouns, processes as verbs, qualities as adjectives, assessments and evaluations as modal verbs, and logical connections as conjunctions. When grammatical metaphor is at work, two meanings are achieved: the grammatical and the semantic (Martin, 2002). According to Halliday (1994), speakers of a language recognize "typical ways of saying things" as well as other possibilities that can be used by a speaker or writer. Typical patterns of wording are what Halliday calls *congruent.* In *incongruent* ways of presenting meaning, the most common change in meaning is from processes (verbs) to nominalizations. In Text One, grammatical metaphor allows the writer to repackage the same meanings using different wording, as in clause 16, where the verb *result* repackages *cause.*

Elaboration in Text One is achieved through repetition and synonymy. The word *split* in clause 1 is repeated in clause 4. We can recognize repetition even when the lexical items are not presented in the same morphological form. Words such as *important* and *importance* are considered repetitions, even though they have different morphological forms. *Synonymy* occurs when a lexical item is synonymous with a preceding one. In Text One, *divided* in clause 14 is synonymous with *split* in clause 1. Table 4.3 presents the clauses and elaboration of meanings in Text One. The main semantic notions that are elaborated are presented in bold.

**TABLE 4.3   Elaboration in Text One**

| Clauses | Elaboration of Meanings | | |
|---|---|---|---|
| 1–3 | **split into 3 branches** | **too much power** | **causing people to get angry** |
| | *Elaboration through repetition* | *Elaboration through synonymy* | |
| 4–5 | they needed to split ⩔ the powers | To keep the power ⩔ balanced | |
| | *Elaboration by specifying* | | |
| | each branch had ⩔ an equal amount of power through checks and balance | | |
| | *Elaboration through synonymy* | *Elaboration through repetition* | *Elaboration through synonymy* |
| 14–15 | If the government ⩔ was not divided into three branches, | the government ⩔ would have too much power and control over people | It may result to ⩔ chaos to everyone. |

## Logical Relationships

Another important linguistic element is the realization of logical relationships. Logical meanings include relationships of time, addition, comparison, and consequence (Martin & Rose, 2003). Logical relationships can be realized between clauses or within a clause. Logical connections between clauses and other stretches of discourse are typically marked through conjunctions (Martin & Rose, 2003). They are used to sequence in time, add, compare, and explain causes, conditions, and purposes (Martin & Rose, 2003). In addition, through grammatical metaphor, logical connections can also be made within the clause through circumstances, verbs, and nouns. An example would be the verb *causing* in clause 3, which expresses causality and a relationship between clauses 2 and 3. Different types of conjunctions are found in Text One. These include additive conjunctions (*and*), comparison indicating contrast (*but*), and consequential conjunctions indicating cause (*because*) and condition (*if*).

Clause 1 has two important textual themes that are consequential markers of cause and condition. Right after the writer's answer to the prompt question, the conjunction *because* indicates the basis for the writer's position, presented in the interpersonal theme *I guess so*. This textual theme is followed by another textual theme, *if*, which introduces a conditional clause that suggests the basis on which the writer's perspective is justified. The textual theme *if* appears again in clause 10 of paragraph three: *If any new rule is passed, it must be followed*. This textual theme is used to introduce a real condition that elaborates on the responsibility of the legislative branch. *If* is also found as a textual theme in clauses 14 and 15 in the conclusion of the text: *If the government was not divided into three branches, the government would have too much power and control over people*. This conditional clause is used to reiterate the writer's thesis presented in clauses 1, 2, and 3 in paragraph one with the same sentence structure: *if the government had not been split into 3 branches, they would have too much power causing people to get angry*. The textual theme *because* occurs again in the last paragraph in *It is also a good thing the government is divided because they can get pretty stupid*. The writer here presents more support for the position that the division of government is appropriate. In Text One, we see the marked theme *To keep the power balanced* in clause 4. This is a non-finite clause that shows a consequential relationship of purpose and suggests a purpose for the split of powers.

Other linguistic resources can bring in similar meanings. Logical connections in academic registers are often realized through nouns and verbs (Halliday & Matthiessen, 2004). This is another example of grammatical metaphor, operating with the logical relationships in a text. In Text One, the causal verb *causing* in clause 3 establishes a causal relationship between clauses 2 and 3. Similarly, the non-finite clause that is a marked theme in clause 4, *To keep the power balanced*, signals a consequential link of purpose. In clause 14, the verb *result* also constructs a causal relationship established between clauses 13 and 14. In these examples, the conjunctive relationships are integrated into the clause, unlike the other relationships expressed between clauses through conjunctions. Conjunctions are a common way to express logical connections in interactional discourse, while nouns and verbs are more commonly used in written discourse to express the same connections (Martin, 1983; Schleppegrell, 2004).

---

## *Reference*

The system of cohesion is especially important in these 8th-grade texts. Markers of cohesion are lexicogrammatical resources for expressing and signaling relations between parts of texts (Halliday & Matthiessen, 2004). *Cohesive resources* are often found in theme position, referring backward to something already presented or referring forward to what is to come.

Reference is a cohesive resource through which pronouns and demonstratives (such as *this* and *that*) are used to refer to parts in or outside of the text (Halliday & Hasan, 1976). Pronouns are a common reference marker and are used to substitute for nouns in discourse. Pronouns are textual resources involving how discourse is presented to the reader and can package sections of meaning to play a new role as the text develops (Martin & Rose, 2003). Two main types of pronouns are seen in the texts. Personal pronouns include those that are determinative (serving as Head in the nominal group, such as *they* in clause 2) or possessive (such as *their* in *their power*). The system of reference interacts with the rheme to theme movement. In the 8th-grade texts analyzed in this chapter, many reference markers in theme position are used to move from rheme to theme.

### Pronouns as Rheme to Theme Movement Resources

The writer of Text One draws on pronouns as a resource for rheme to theme movement, using this resource to present and organize the information. The writer introduces new information in a clause rheme that is then picked up again in a subsequent clause theme. Most of the resources used for this textual move are pronouns, with the exception of the theme *To keep the power balanced* in clause 4, which picks up the word *power* introduced in the rheme in clause 2.

In clause 1, *3 branches* is introduced in rheme position, then picked up by the pronoun *they* in clause 2. The pronominal reference marker *They* appears in clause 7 and refers backward to *the House of Representatives and the Senate*, which occur in rheme position in clause 6. The pronoun *it* in clause 16 is again used to refer back to the rheme of clause 15, *would have too much power and control over people.* This use of pronouns enables the writer to condense information by presenting it as clause theme and move the discourse forward with new information in the rheme.

### Confusion Around Pronoun Reference

There are some examples of confusion around pronoun reference in Text One. We see several reference markers that appear in theme position. The first pronominal reference marker *They* appears in theme position in the first paragraph, in *They made sure each branch had an equal amount of power through checks and balances* and is a reference outside of the text to *the framers of the Constitution*, which occurs in the essay prompt. The writer should have identified the framers of the Constitution the first time this term was used. Another pronominal reference that caused confusion was *it*, which appears in theme position in clause 8 and refers to *laws*. This was an inappropriate choice because *it* was in the singular form instead of the plural (*they*), showing the confusion that pronoun use can cause even to writers who are considered more successful. *They* occurs again in clause 18, *because they can get pretty stupid*, but this pronominal reference is unclear. It may be a reference to *government* (or people in government), which occurs in the previous clause. A similar reference occurs in the opening clauses of the first paragraph, clauses 1, 2, and 3: *because if the government had not been split into 3 branches, <u>they</u> would have too much power causing people to get angry*, with *they* referring back to *government*. Pronominal reference in theme position can be a useful strategy in building cohesive texts, but it may cause some ambiguity and confusion as to what exactly the pronouns are referring to.

The writer of Text One uses a variety of linguistic resources to construct this essay. Even though the student confused some of the constituents of each branch, the student shows a clear idea of the system of checks and balances and is able to name the different branches and use some historical knowledge to build the essay. The student is also able to use some historical terminology such as *the House of Representatives, the Senate, the Supreme Court,* and *the government.*

## The Linguistic Constructs at Work: Text Two

Text Two is another example of a highly valued essay. According to Jerry, the 8th-grade teacher who assessed this text, Text Two is an example of a successful essay. Jerry's assessment of the student's essay can be demonstrated by the analysis of the linguistic features of the essay. The analysis shows how certain language resources construe a highly valued text. This essay was considered especially effective due to its organization and overall structure. The thematic analysis of Text Two is presented in Table 4.4 following the presentation of the essay.

---

### TEXT TWO

The framers of the Constitution were successful in achieving a balance of power. They achieved this balance of power because they made three different branches and they had responsibilities that balanced each other.

The branches were the legislative, executive branch, and the judicial branch. The executive branch which is the president, vice president, and the Governor has a different responsibility like they approve the law. That is only one of the responsibility they have.

The legislative branch writes the law. In the legislative branch is the Congress. Their responsibility balances the executive and the judicial branch. Like for a bill to become a law it must first pass through the houses of Congress then go through the other branches.

The judicial branch has the Supreme Court. Their responsibility also balances the other two branches. For a bill they hear witness and examine the bill clause by clause.

The Constitution wanted everyone to be equal, even the government. The branches have the same power and their responsibilities balance out each other. One branch does not have more control or power than the other. So, no branch dominates and controls the other two. This was an important aspect for the Constitution because it was the organization of government. This was successful and the three branches were created with equal power and control.

---

**TABLE 4.4   Thematic Analysis of Text Two**

| Clause # | Textual | Topical | Rheme |
|---|---|---|---|
| | | **Theme** | |
| 1. | | **The framers of the Constitution** | were successful in achieving a balance of power. |
| 2. | | **They** | achieved this balance of power |
| 3. | **because** | **they** | made three different branches |
| 4. | **and** | **they** | had responsibilities that balanced each other. |
| 5. | | **The branches** | were the legislative, executive branch, and the judicial branch. |
| 6. | | **The executive branch which is the president, vice president, and the Governor** | has a different responsibility |
| 7. | **like** | **they** | approve the law. |
| 8. | | **That** | is only one of the responsibility they have. |
| 9. | | **The legislative branch** | writes the law. |
| 10. | | **In the legislative branch*** | is the Congress. |
| 11. | | **Their responsibility** | balances the executive and the judicial branch. |
| 12. | **Like** | **for a bill to become a law*** | it must first pass through the houses of Congress then go through the other branches. |

**TABLE 4.4 (continued)   Thematic Analysis of Text Two**

| | Theme | | |
|---|---|---|---|
| Clause # | Textual | Topical | Rheme |
| 13. | | The judicial branch | has the Supreme Court. |
| 14. | | Their responsibility | also balances the other two branches. |
| 15. | | For a bill* | they hear witness and examine the bill clause by clause. |
| 16. | | The Constitution | wanted everyone to be equal, even the government. |
| 17. | | The branches | have the same power |
| 18. | and | their responsibilities | balance out each other. |
| 19. | | One branch | does not have more control or power than the other. |
| 20. | So, | no branch | dominates and controls the other two. |
| 21. | | This | was an important aspect for the Constitution |
| 22. | because | it | was the organization of government. |
| 23. | | This | was successful |
| 24. | and | the three branches | were created with equal power and control. |

The writer of Text Two begins the essay by providing an answer to the question posed in the prompt. The writer directly presents the position that will be supported in the essay in clause 1, *The framers of the Constitution were successful in achieving a balance of power.* This is the macro-theme of the essay, which will be developed and supported by subsequent paragraphs. This thesis, according to Jerry, provides a "solid position" on the question. Jerry found this start to be particularly important for the essay construction, since the first clause that the reader sees addresses the question and provides the essay position. According to Jerry, the student "breaks it down literally branch by branch." The overall structure is *thesis, executive branch, legislative branch, judicial branch,* and *conclusion.* The student, in Jerry's view, knows how to structure a 5-paragraph essay. In a similar way as the writer of Text One, the writer of Text Two provides historical information about each of the branch's powers to show how each branch *had responsibilities that balanced each other,* presented in rheme position in clause 4. The introduction is the primary place where the student introduces the notions that are then picked up in the body paragraphs. The first clause of paragraph two names the three branches, which are then defined in paragraphs two, three, and four. Each branch's responsibilities are described, showing the writer's historical understanding. For instance, in paragraph two, the student starts out with the executive branch and cites one responsibility. According to Jerry, the clause *That is only one of the responsibility they have* acknowledges that if the student had more time to write, this writer would develop other responsibilities, which Jerry assesses as "good." Even though the writer confuses some of the responsibilities, most of the historical information is accurate. The conclusion comes back to the point of power and responsibilities. The last clause mirrors the thesis, bringing back the idea that the framers were *successful.*

The thematic choices of Text Two helped the writer structure an essay that was highly valued. The topical themes in paragraph one are held constant. Paragraph one starts with the topical theme *The framers of the Constitution,* which is taken up by the pronominal reference marker *they* in clause 2, which is then used again in the subsequent clause, clause 3. These thematic choices show that the writer selected *The framers of the Constitution* as a point of departure for the introduction. In addition, consequential markers of cause and additive markers appear as textual themes. Clauses 3 and 4 have two important textual themes. *Because* in clause 3, *because they made three different branches,* marks the cause for the achievement of a balance of power. In clause 4, *and they had responsibilities that balanced each other,* the additive marker *and* signals additional information. These textual themes mark the logical relationships to other parts of discourse.

A rheme to theme movement is also found in Text Two. One successful aspect that Jerry found was the structure of the essay, and this is evidenced by the rheme to theme movement in clauses 3, 5, 6, 9, and 13. The rheme of clause 3, *made three different branches,* is picked up by the pronominal reference marker *they* in clause 4. *Three different branches* in the rheme from clause 3 is taken up again in clause 5 as the theme *the branches,* a point of departure for the naming of the branches, which occurs in rheme position. The names of the three branches, *the legislative, executive branch, and the judicial branch,* are introduced in rheme position in clause 5, then each branch is picked up in theme position in clauses 6, 9, and 13. This rheme to theme movement enables the writer to use the branches as a method of development for the essay and to provide a successful essay organization.

In addition, elaboration relationships are also effectively employed in Text Two. Each rheme in paragraph one elaborates the rheme of the preceding clause. For instance, the rheme of clause 1 contains *achieving a balance of power,* which is then restated as *achieved this balance of power* in clause 2.

The demonstrative *this* helps to create the connection between the rhemes. Similarly, the rheme of clause 4 includes *that balanced each other*, where the noun *balance* is now constructed as a verb *balanced* and has an elaborating relationship with clauses 1 and 2. Being able to manipulate the language in these ways through the process of elaboration is a very important aspect of this text, and one that Jerry found particularly relevant.

Paragraph two starts out with an explanation introduced by the topical theme *the branches*. The second clause of paragraph two, clause 6, starts with the topical theme *The executive branch which is the president, vice president, and the Governor*. The topical theme is the entire phrase that contains the embedded clause *which is the president, vice president, and the Governor*. This embedded clause elaborates *the executive branch*; it is a defining relative clause used as part of the characterization of the branch. The word *responsibility* in rheme position in clause 6 takes up the word *responsibilities* presented in rheme position in clause 4. There is also a constant theme realized by the pronoun *they* in clause 7 that refers back to the theme of clause 6, *the executive branch*. Clause 7 starts with the textual theme *like*, which introduces an example of the responsibility in the theme of clause 6. This clause elaborates on clause 6 by exemplifying it. As Jerry pointed out, the textual theme *like* functions as a *for example* and is an example of a spoken feature in written language. According to Jerry, students "write the way they talk." *Responsibility* is used again in rheme position in clause 8. The use of the word *responsibility* in several clauses of this text helps to make this text cohesive. In clause 8, we see the first instance of the use of the demonstrative *that* as a rheme to theme development from clause 7. Demonstratives are a useful resource for rheme to theme movement because they enable packaging of a lot of information in a single word, and they are often used in conclusions.

The topical theme *The legislative branch* introduces paragraph three. Information about the legislative branch is presented in the rest of this paragraph. Clause 10 starts with the marked theme *In the legislative branch,* a theme that establishes location and enables the writer to maintain a constant theme. *Their responsibility* in clause 11 presents the work of the legislative branch, the *balance*, which is then elaborated and exemplified in clause 12 with the marked theme *for a bill to become a law*. The elaborating clause, starting with the word *like*, is used to exemplify the work of the legislative branch. As Jerry stated, this *like* functions as a *for example*. Paragraph four, like paragraph three, starts out with a branch as the topical theme, *The judicial branch*, in clause 13. Clause 14, like clause 11 of the previous paragraph, starts with the topical theme *Their responsibility* and again brings up the point about *balance*, a key point of development in this essay. The rheme to theme movement helps the writer elaborate on the clauses previously presented, such as in clause 14, where *their responsibility* picks up on *responsibilities* presented in rheme position in clause 4 of the introduction and *responsibility* in clauses 6 and 8 in paragraph two. The semantic notion of *responsibility* is used throughout the essay in several paragraphs to establish the idea of balance. The repetition of this word helps the writer to talk about the work of each branch to support the meanings presented in clause 4, *and they had responsibilities that balanced each other*. Clause 15 has a marked theme, *for a bill*, which is similar to the theme of clause 12, *for a bill to become a law*. In addition, the words *the other branches* in clause 12 and *the other two branches* in clause 14 refer to *the executive and the judicial branch* in clause 11. In short, the thematic choices of paragraphs three and four are functional for the presentation of new information in rheme position. These choices are also very cohesive, which is evidenced by the many similarities between the themes of each paragraph.

The topical theme that starts the essay conclusion, *The Constitution*, takes up the topical theme that introduced the essay, *The framers of the Constitution*. The consequential marker of cause *because* is used again in clause 24, *because it was the organization of government*, to show that the Constitution established the organization of government. The consequential marker *So* in clause 20 shows a consequence for what is presented in clause 19, *One branch does not have more control or power than the other*. The consequential meaning helps the writer construct the notion of *balance* by making a logical connection and establishing an elaborating relationship between the two clauses. In addition, there are two rheme to theme textual moves in the conclusion: in clause 22, where *it* refers to *the Constitution*, and in the last clause of the essay, where the demonstrative *this* in theme position in clause 23 picks up the rheme of clause 22. This textual move enables the writer to make links and draw conclusions. Jerry, commenting on this paragraph, points out that the "concept is there." Referring to clauses 19 and 20, Jerry affirms that he "likes that" because these are nice concluding sentences that wrap up the thesis. In addition, Jerry finds the final clauses 23 and 24 particularly effective because they go back to the original thesis and affirm that success was achieved. Jerry concludes that "it's strong for that reason," giving particular emphasis to the importance of reiterating the thesis in the conclusion. According to Jerry, the student is demonstrating some historical understanding.

Table 4.5 presents constant theme and rheme to theme movement in Text Two. Like in table 4.2, double-sided arrows indicate rheme to theme movement. One-sided and straight arrows show constant themes.

**TABLE 4.5  Constant Theme, Rheme to Theme Movement: Text Two**

| Clause # | Topical | Rheme |
|---|---|---|
| 1. | The framers of the Constitution | were successful in achieving a balance of power. |
| 2. | They | achieved this balance of power |
| 3. | they | made three different branches |
| 4. | they | had responsibilities that balanced each other. |
| 5. | The branches | were the legislative, executive branch, and the judicial branch. |
| 6. | The executive branch which is the president, vice president, and the Governor | has a different responsibility |
| 7. | they | approve the law. |
| 8. | That | is only one of the responsibility they have. |
| 9. | The legislative branch | writes the law. |
| 10. | In the legislative branch* | is the Congress. |
| 11. | Their responsibility | balances the executive and the judicial branch. |
| 12. | for a bill to become a law* | it must first pass through the houses of Congress then go through the other branches. |
| 13. | The judicial branch | has the Supreme Court. |
| 14. | Their responsibility | also balances the other two branches. |
| 15. | For a bill* | they hear witness and examine the bill clause by clause. |
| 16. | The Constitution | wanted everyone to be equal, even the government. |
| 17. | The branches | have the same power |
| 18. | their responsibilities | balance out each other. |
| 19. | One branch | does not have more control or power than the other. |
| 20. | no branch | dominates and controls the other two. |
| 21. | This | was an important aspect for the Constitution |
| 22. | it | was the organization of government. |
| 23. | This | was successful |
| 24. | the three branches | were created with equal power and control. |

As Jerry highlighted, the entire concluding paragraph takes the reader back to the essay introduction. This is accomplished through elaboration. Two key semantic notions are elaborated, *balance* and *equality*. Clauses 17, 18, 19, and 20 in the conclusion are an elaboration of *balance of power*, presented in rheme position in clauses 1 and 2. In the introduction, the *balance of power* is restated through the lexical choices *balance out each other* (clause 18), *does not have more control or power than the other* (clause 19), and *dominates and controls the other two* (clause 20). The semantic notion of equality is also present in the essay, with *be equal* (clause 16), *have the same power* (clause 17), and *equal power and control* (clause 24). Here we also see the repetition of several words such as *power* and *control* that work to reinforce the ideas presented in the macro-theme. In addition, the verb *made* in clause 3 is restated as *were created* in clause 24. These lexical choices all contribute to the overall reinstatement of the message presented in the macro-theme and help the writer re-establish the historical information. Furthermore, the word *responsibility* appears in rheme position in clauses 4, 6, and 8 and is then picked up in theme position in clauses 11, 14, and 18, occurring in every paragraph of the essay. The adjective *successful* in the macro-theme (clause 1) is also repeated in clause 23 of the conclusion. While clauses 17, 18, 19, and 20 show very similar meanings, the restatements provide the kind of elaboration that enables the writer to reinforce ideas previously presented. The last two clauses of the conclusion, according to Jerry, were particularly important for reiterating the macro-theme. In addition, several words in theme and rheme position from the introduction are reiterated in the conclusion, making this text very cohesive and, according to Jerry, elaborated and developed. Elaboration was a major linguistic resource used in Text Two, presented in Table 4.5. The conclusion is basically an elaboration and reiteration of ideas already presented. These function as catalysts for the confirmation of the historical information that has been presented in the essay.

Jerry stated that if the student had gone one step further in terms of the historical information, this essay would have been "a much stronger essay." Jerry's overall assessment, however, was that this essay was successful compared to the others that he had read. Jerry also stressed the importance of considering this a rough draft in some ways, since it was a timed assignment that students had to complete with their historical knowledge and without consulting any sources. Jerry believes that "if this was a rough draft, and if I went over this with the student, sent her home to do research, open book, she'd probably come back with something very strong," suggesting the writer's potential for improvement and recognizing the challenges of timed writing.

Table 4.6 presents the clauses and elaboration of meanings in Text Two. The main semantic notions that are elaborated are presented in bold.

**TABLE 4.6    Elaboration in Text Two**

Clauses   Elaboration of Meanings

| Clauses | | | |
|---|---|---|---|
| 1 | were successful | in achieving a balance of power | |
| | | *Elaboration through repetition* | |
| 2–3 | | achieved this balance of power | |
| | | *Elaboration through repetition* | |
| 4 | | had responsibilities that balanced each other. | |
| 16 | | | wanted everyone to be equal, even the government. |
| | | | *Elaboration through synonymy* |
| 17 | | | have the same power |
| | | *Elaboration through repetition* | |
| 18 | | balance out each other. | |
| | | *Elaboration through synonymy* | |
| 19 | | does not have more control or power than the other. | |
| | | *Elaboration through synonymy* | |
| 20 | | dominates and controls the other two | |
| | *Elaboration through repetition* | | *Elaboration through repetition* |
| 23 | was successful | | were created with equal power and control. |

---

*Summary*

The texts just presented were considered effective. These writers' choices in the areas of thematic development and cohesion contribute to the realization of a register that was considered appropriate for the exposition genre. Through the thematic choices, the writers signaled the organizational structure and created a highly structured text organized around the three branches, with each branch serving as the point of departure of the body paragraphs. Cohesive resources such as pronouns were used to make links and establish relationships between elements of discourse. Elaborating relationships were established to reiterate the main semantic notions present in the texts. The most distinguishing feature between the two essays that made Text Two more successful than Text One was the use of elaboration as a linguistic resource to reiterate points made throughout the essay. Elaboration was present in Text One, but Text Two utilized it more systematically and more often. As the analysis demonstrated, this strategy was highly valued by the 8th-grade teachers. The thematic choices of Text Two helped realize an organizational structure of *thesis, executive branch, legislative branch, judicial branch,* and *conclusion.* It was Jerry's opinion that the student knew how to structure a 5-paragraph essay effectively. The writer of Text Two also shows a certain facility with language that enabled the presentation of information in different ways through the use of repetition and synonymy.

While this section highlighted samples of more successful writers and the language features that they draw on when they write, the following section focuses on second language learners' writing. We turn now to examples of two ELLs. Text Three is an example of an essay that needs improvement on both content and process of writing. Text Four was considered a strong essay. The analyses of these two essays show the language choices that the students made and suggest resources that still need to be developed.

## English Language Learners

This section of the chapter focuses on the writing of mainstreamed ELLs. The teachers identified these texts as being written by ELLs. Rather than highlighting students' language errors, an approach that has been the focus of much English as a Second Language pedagogy in recent years (e.g., Ferris & Roberts, 2001), the analysis considers ELLs' language choices and the linguistic resources that they rely on to write.

### *Example of an Essay in Need of Improvement*

Text Three was assessed as in need of improvement and was considered to be an example of an essay that needs further development. According to Jerry, this student needs to further develop historical understanding regarding the Constitution. I present Jerry's assessment of the essay in the context of the linguistic analysis.

---

### TEXT THREE

The branch that has more power. I think that one branch does have more power than the other. The executive branch has more power because nothing in this whole world is perfect and balanced right. And I think it's the executive branch because that's the branch that controls the army and the president.

And yes the farmers did get their check because it's their right to get paid for on what they done to deserve it and respect on what they do. And the three branches have the power to not give their checks but also has power to give their checks too. So they always have a decision to make checks and balances but always one branch has more power than another one.

And that's not all they check and balance they also check and balance schools, houses, companies, stores, and other important things like food, people, drivers license, jobs, automotive, etc. The government has already important job and they must do it making money (treasury), making laws or bills.

I think the government has the most complicated job and they have to be energetic be ready for anything to happen and it's up for the people too, not just them.

---

The writer puts forth a position that addresses the essay question in *I think that one branch does have more power than the other.* The reason given after this assertion is a generalized idea not based on historical information. However, in the last clause of the introduction, the writer shows some historical understanding by saying that the executive branch includes the president and the army, even though, as Jerry mentioned, this assertion is not completely accurate. Table 4.7 presents the thematic analysis of Text Three.

Unlike Text Two, Text Three does not start out with an answer to the question posed in the prompt. The opening, *The branch that has more power,* is an incomplete clause that Jerry found problematic. This states the topic of the essay but does not function as a thesis. Clauses 2, 3, and 4 are the macro-theme of the text: *I think that one branch does have more power than the other. The executive branch has more power because nothing in this whole world is perfect and balanced right.* These clauses summarize the writer's position on the topic, although it is not developed as in the other essays. Jerry finds this problematic because it takes the writer three clauses to get to the main point of his essay. There is also an issue with the reason given to justify the writer's position, marked by the consequential marker *because* in clause 4, *because nothing in this whole world is perfect and balanced right.* This causal relationship between clause 3, *the executive branch has more power,* and the clause *nothing in this whole world is perfect and balanced right* presented in clause 4 is

**TABLE 4.7  Thematic Analysis of Text Three**

| Clause # | Theme | | | Rheme |
|---|---|---|---|---|
| | Textual | Interpersonal | Topical | |
| 1. | | | The branch | that has more power. |
| 2. | | I think that | one branch | does have more power than the other. |
| 3. | | | The executive branch | has more power |
| 4. | because | | nothing in this whole world | is perfect and balanced right. |
| 5. | And | I think | it | 's the executive branch |
| 6. | because | | that | 's the branch that controls the army and the president. |
| 7. | And | yes | the farmers | did get their check |
| 8. | because | | it | 's their right to get paid for on what they done to deserve it and respect on what they do. |
| 9. | And | | the three branches | have the power to not give their checks |
| 10. | but | | [the three branches] | also has power to give their checks too. |
| 11. | So | | they | always have a decision to make checks and balances |
| 12. | but | always | one branch | has more power than another one. |
| 13. | And | | that | 's not all they check and balance |
| 14. | | | they | also check and balance schools, houses, companies, stores, and other important things like food, people, drivers license, jobs, automotive, etc. |
| 15. | | | The government | has already important job |
| 16. | and | | they | must do it making money (treasury), making laws or bills. |
| 17. | | I think | the government | has the most complicated job |
| 18. | and | | they | have to be energetic be ready for anything to happen |
| 19. | and | | it | 's up for the people too, not just them. |

not based on historical information, making the writer's position ineffective. The cause presented by the writer is a generalized statement that does not clarify the writer's assertion in clause 3. Unlike Texts One and Two, Text Three does not address each branch's power in the body paragraphs. Jerry affirms that this is a good example of "writing in a speaking style." According to him, the student repeats things over and over again.

The thematic choices of paragraph one show the student's difficulties with development in this essay. We see in paragraph one that the first three themes are not related to each other or to rhemes of preceding clauses, except in the case of the demonstrative *that* in clause 6, which picks up the rheme of clause 5. Most of the themes of paragraph one do not function as constant themes in the way we saw in earlier essays. This introductory paragraph does not identify the points to be made in the essay, nor is it organized to signal them. According to Jerry, there is also a question of relevance to the prompt; in this paragraph, the student expressed a few things about the executive branch, but nothing at all about whether the balance of power works. Jerry believes that this student does not understand these historical concepts and while the student has an idea, the three-and-a-half sentences the student takes to get to it in this paragraph indicate to him that this writer may not have understood the prompt completely.

The topical themes of paragraph two are not related to each other or to the rhemes of preceding clauses. The paragraph starts out with the textual theme *and*. For this writer, *and* seems to function as an organizing device indicating *addition* as it introduces each new paragraph. The interpersonal theme *yes* construes interaction with the reader, contributing to the creation of a writing style that resembles speaking.

The logical connections in the text are marked explicitly through conjunctions. The consequential conjunctions *because* and *so*, which mark causal relationships, occur in clauses 8 and 11. Two adversative conjunctions (*but*) occur in clauses 10 and 12. These conjunctive resources help the writer make links between clauses. The main problem with paragraph two is that it presents content that is unrelated to the introduction. The information presented in paragraph two was not relevant to a discussion of the division of power in the Constitution. As Jerry pointed out, the writer confuses *framers* and *farmers* in clauses 7 and 8. In addition, the student confuses the term *check* in the historical concept of *checks and balances* (the system established by the Constitution to prevent any branch of government from becoming too powerful) with the everyday meaning of *check* (a written order instructing a bank to pay money). These, Jerry says, are "obvious weaknesses." *The three branches* appears as theme in clause 9, bringing the discussion back to the division of government in the Constitution. However, these are just assertions with no historical information to support them.

Paragraph three again begins with the textual theme *and*. As in paragraph two, this conjunction makes a link between paragraphs. The paragraph shows confusion about the role of the federal government, evidenced by the information provided in the rheme of clause 14. According to Jerry, the student brings up some things that are correct. For instance, schools are a government function, while houses are a function of the private housing market and also the federal program known as Section 8 housing. As Jerry stated, "Somewhere deep down, this person understands what they're trying to say but can't get it out right." According to Jerry, the student might be trying to say that "it's important to have a check and balance on government because the government is involved in some aspects in people's lives," but as readers we cannot really tell if that is what the student is saying. The writer, according to Jerry, is saying "that the government has an important job, and is strongly implying that it affects everybody's daily life," as in clause 15, where *the government* is the point of departure. This thematic choice of clause 15 is kept constant in four consecutive clauses so that the writer is able talk about the government functions, including two clauses in paragraph four. This constant theme helps the writer develop the text from one angle and add new information in the rheme of each clause.

The language choices of this writer indicate some confusion about the role of the federal government. Jerry finds that

> maybe the analysis that's not there would be because it's so important, because we live in a democracy, because the government has its hands in all these areas of our lives, it's vital that the people retain control of it, not let it get out of hand, not turn it into a dictatorship. That's the implied argument there, but it's never stated or even gotten close to.

In paragraph four, the conclusion of the essay, instead of elaborating on what has already been presented in the introduction and the body paragraphs, the writer is adding completely new information for the text in the rheme, not meeting the normal expectations for content placement and organizational structure for the expository essay.

The thematic choices of this essay do not follow a certain pattern to help the writer structure the content of the text. The topical themes, for example, in paragraphs one, two, and three show that the writer does not follow a constant theme or a rheme to theme movement as patterns of development, found in Texts One and Two.

Several interpersonal themes are present in Text Three. The interpersonal theme *I think* is used three times in Text Three, twice in the introduction and once in the conclusion. The four focus history teachers mentioned that this feature of students' writing is not a valued one because history should be written from a less "personal perspective," which choices such as *I think* and *I believe* do not help to construct. The writers' language choices help construct a text that, in teachers' views, is "subjective."

Cohesive resources, especially pronominal reference, occur throughout this text, but only once do we find a rheme to theme movement, with the demonstrative *that* in clause 6, which refers back to *the executive branch* in the rheme of clause 5. Several other pronouns are used throughout the essay, such as *their* in clauses 7, 9, and 10 and *they* in clauses 8 and 13. The writer shows some knowledge of pronominal reference and demonstrative use that could be strengthened by attention to how these cohesive resources can help structure a text in a more effective way.

Resources for elaborating are also present in Text Three. Clause 12, for instance, is a restatement of clause 2. But this restatement appears in paragraph 4. As we have seen in the stronger essays, elaborating clauses are typically found in the conclusion and used as resources that bring out the meanings presented in the introduction and supported by the historical information of body paragraphs.

The overall logical connections made in this text realize a movement from clause to clause in what Jerry describes as "writing in a speaking style." This "speaking style" is evidenced, for example, by the many conjunctions (*and*) serving as textual themes that construct an essay that resembles spoken language as it has been described by functional linguists (e.g., Schleppegrell, 2001; 2004). The conjunction *and* has a wider range of semantic functions in spoken texts; it may show temporal sequence, consequence, comparison, or addition (Schleppegrell, 2001). Although typically an additive conjunction, *and* in Text Three actually links clauses with adversative relationships in 13 and 19. These relationships would typically be realized by *but* or *however* in more academic texts. In addition to the conjunction *and*, the consequential markers of cause *because* and *so* help the writer build causal structures in the text. Martin (1989) suggests that marking a causal relation between two clauses with a conjunction such as *because* and *so* is a very common way of reasoning in spoken language, which gives this text a hortatory style. In fact, out of the 19 clauses present in this text, 13 are marked by conjunctive relationships, helping to build this hortatory discourse style and constructing a text that resembles spoken language. Contributing to this resemblance is also the use of the interpersonal themes that express the writer's attitude explicitly. The collection of lexical and grammatical features of Text Three produces an interactional style.

The different choices made by the writer have an overall effect on the meaning and effectiveness of the text. The writer clearly needs to develop a repertoire of resources for expressing historical understanding. Drawing on the familiar language of informal interaction in a context that is much more academic, this mainstreamed ELL produces a text that is considered by the teacher in need of further development. In addition, this student clearly used his knowledge of everyday vocabulary by incorrectly reading *farmers* instead of *framers* and *check* as a written order given to a bank instead of as part of the historical concept of *checks and balances*. The writer is certainly drawing on his everyday knowledge to realize an academic register and needs to develop historical understanding about the division of power in the Constitution. Jerry states that the essay "suggests a central idea, but doesn't state it, just implies it." As Jerry mentioned, this writing has potential: "Somewhere deep down, this person understands what they're trying to say but can't get it out right." This also shows that the way in which students' ideas are presented and expressed can produce texts that do not conform to academic expectations.

## Example of a Successful Essay: Text Four

Being an ELL does not mean being a weak writer. This text, also written by a mainstreamed ELL, is an example of an essay considered effective by the teacher.

---

**TEXT FOUR**

I think the framers of the constitution were successfully achieving a balance of power. Executive branch is the president, vice president and the cabinet. The legislative branch is the Senate and the House of Representatives. The last branch is the Judicial Branch and it includes the United States Supreme Court, Appellate, trial courts and other federal courts. Those three branches had almost the same powers.

The most important branch was the executive branch because it was the one who executed the laws the legislative branch made. Also, judicial branch was the one studied and interpreted the law. None of them gained too much power because they were friendly and were in peace doing their jobs.

I think no one got too much power because the president George Washington didn't want to be president but people chose him and they liked him a lot. So everyone had equal rights and no one gained too much power. In the constitution there was a law that didn't let the government gain too much power.

---

The 8th-grade teacher, Tom, considered this essay effective, and almost a 3 in a 4-point scale, because it "at least tries to get somewhere." Tom found it particularly important that the student repeats constantly how the branch works. Table 4.8 presents the thematic analysis of Text Four.

Paragraph one starts out with an interpersonal theme, *I think*, which presents the writer's thesis, the macro-theme of the essay: *I think the framers of the constitution were successfully achieving a balance of power*. This paragraph presents and names the three branches, introducing each with the topical themes *executive branch, the legislative branch*, and *the last branch*. Clauses 2 and 3 define the executive and legislative branch. Clause 4, introduced by the topical theme *the last branch*, identifies the judicial branch, which is then defined in clause 5, initiated by the additive marker *and*. The pronoun *it* in clause 5 reveals a rheme to theme movement, referring to *the judicial branch* in rheme position in clause 4. The last clause of the paragraph, clause 6, starts with the theme *those three branches*, which functions as a reference back to the themes of the previous clauses, indicated by the demonstrative *those*. This was a particularly effective use of the demonstrative as a cohesive resource linking the themes. Information presented in the rheme of clause 6 is developed in paragraph two, which focuses on the powers of each branch.

Paragraph two starts out with *the most important branch*, which is named in the rheme as *the executive branch*. Clause 8 presents the justification for such assessment, introduced by the textual theme and consequential marker of cause *because*. Here we also see a rheme to theme movement in the use of the pronoun *it* referring back to *the executive branch* presented in rheme position in clause 7. The rheme of clause 8 presents both the power of the executive branch and the power of the legislative branch. The internal connector *Also* in clause 9 is used to add to the description of the powers of the *judicial branch*, with the topical theme naming the branch whose responsibility is developed in rheme position. Clauses 10 and 11 conclude paragraph two, bringing back the idea of *balance of power*.

Paragraph three starts out with an elaborating clause, clause 12, which brings the paragraph back again to the macro-theme of the essay. The interpersonal theme *I think* is used again in this clause, also used in the macro-theme (clause 1). A consequential marker of cause introduces clause 13, which presents a reason for the position presented in the previous clause. This reason, according to Tom, is invalid, but presents some historical information that could be elaborated. Tom found this paragraph particularly relevant because, in talking about George Washington, the student is "trying to give a reason, trying to set up some causality there even though it is an

**TABLE 4.8  Thematic Analysis of Text Four**

| | | Theme | | |
|---|---|---|---|---|
| Clause # | Textual | Interpersonal | Topical | Rheme |
| 1. | | I think | the framers of the constitution | were successfully achieving a balance of power. |
| 2. | | | Executive branch | is the president, vice president and the cabinet. |
| 3. | | | The legislative branch | is the Senate and the House of Representatives. |
| 4. | | | The last branch | is the Judicial Branch |
| 5. | and | | it | includes the United States Supreme Court, Appellate, trial courts and other federal courts. |
| 6. | | | Those three branches | had almost the same powers. |
| 7. | | | The most important branch | was the executive branch |
| 8. | because | | it | was the one who executed the laws the legislative branch made. |
| 9. | Also, | | judicial branch | was the one studied and interpreted the law. |
| 10. | | | None of them | gained too much power |
| 11. | because | | they | were friendly and were in peace doing their jobs. |
| 12. | | | no one | got too much power |
| 13. | because | I think | the president George Washington | didn't want to be president |
| 14. | but | | people | chose him |
| 15. | and | | they | liked him a lot. |
| 16. | So | | everyone | had equal rights |
| 17. | and | | no one | gained too much power. |
| 18. | | | In the constitution* | there was a law that didn't let the government gain too much power. |

**TABLE 4.9   Elaboration in Text Four**

| Clauses | Elaboration of Meanings |
| --- | --- |
| 1 | **achieving a balance of power** |
| | *Elaboration through synonymy* |
| 10 | gained too much power |
| | *Elaboration through repetition* |
| 12 | got too much power |
| | *Elaboration through synonymy* |
| 16 | had equal rights |
| | *Elaboration through synonymy* |
| 17 | gained too much power |
| | *Elaboration through repetition* |
| 18 | gain too much power |

invalid reason" and "showing that glimmer for giving a reason." Tom finds that the student is "at least thinking about the question there." Clauses 17 and 18, like clauses 10 and 12, restate the macro-theme. Tom found clause 18 particularly appropriate because the writer is bringing in historical information from the first three articles of the Constitution and "restating what he said up there," that is, in the macro-theme of the essay.

This essay uses several elaborating relationships. The semantic notion *balance of power* is developed and reiterated throughout the essay. For instance, we see this notion being reiterated and elaborated in clauses 10, 12, 16, 17, and 18. Table 4.9 presents the clauses and elaboration of meanings in Text Four. The main semantic notions that are elaborated are presented in bold.

## Discussion

### *Expectations for the Expository Writing Task*

The writers whose texts were featured in this chapter have drawn on different language resources to construct essays that were assessed as more or less appropriate demonstrations of the exposition genre. The two 8th-grade history teachers who assessed these essays had clear expectations for students' writing, and even though they differed in some of these expectations, there were major similarities that could be identified.

The ability to explain each branch was considered particularly important for students' demonstration of their historical understanding. The

**TABLE 4.10  Expectations for the Construction of the Expository Genre**

| Rhetorical Term | Social Function |
| --- | --- |
| 1. Thesis (Macro-theme) | to provide the writer's position on a topic (thesis answers the question posed in prompt) |
| 2. Position with historical information | to support the thesis |
| 3. Reinforcement of the thesis | to emphasize and reiterate the writer's position |

writer's ability to remember different tasks that each branch has was an expectation of the 8th-grade teachers. In addition to specific content expectations, teachers highlighted what they expected in terms of organization.

The essay prompt calls for the student to present a position. Student writers, then, need to use grammatical choices that present evaluation and judgment in an authoritative way (Schleppegrell, 2004). As shown in Table 4.10, both 8th-grade teachers agreed that to answer the question posed in the prompt, students would need to provide a *thesis* that presented the writer's position on the question, historical information as foundation for the position, and a restatement of the thesis to reiterate the writer's point.

Teachers have expectations for the completion of writing tasks that often remain implicit. Even when teachers ask students to "take a stance" or "present their ideas clearly," the linguistic resources which realize these tasks often remain implied. As presented in this chapter, teachers do have expectations for how a thesis should be presented and historical information included in expository writing. This chapter showed how these expectations are realized in the language that students bring to the task.

## Differences Between More and Less Effective Texts

Specific features from the more and less effective texts can be highlighted. Certainly, talking about these features in isolation is somewhat challenging because it is the collection of linguistic choices that enables us to understand how the essays are constructed.

The more effective essays featured in this chapter shared some common linguistic features. They used thematic choices as a way to organize their essays effectively. Both constant theme and rheme to theme development resources were observed in the texts. In particular, in body paragraphs we saw a constant theme with each branch in theme position so that a description or explanation about each branch could be included in the rheme. In addition, in a rheme to theme movement, information presented in rheme position was picked up by subsequent themes, through the effective use of demonstratives, pronouns, and other nominal groups, with the rhemes of introductory clauses serving as organizing devices for the rest of the essay, as in Texts One and Two. In this chapter, there were several examples of confusion around pronoun reference. Even the writers whose texts were considered "strong" had some difficulty with pronoun usage. Pronominal reference in theme position can be a useful strategy in building cohesive texts, but it may cause some ambiguity and confusion as to what exactly the pronouns are referring to. Text structuring and organization can be a focus of pedagogy; in particular, students can learn how to move from rheme to theme effectively through the use of condensation strategies such as demonstratives, pronominal reference, and other linguistic strategies that functional linguists have identified, such as nominalization. Nominalization, which displays information that has been presented in verbs and whole clauses as nouns, is functional for a rheme to theme movement. Nominalization is a more sophisticated use of the rheme to theme development (Schleppegrell, 2004).

Following one of the key expectations of teachers for addressing the prompt question directly, the essays that were more highly valued presented a clear thesis that basically reworded the question posed in the prompt as a position, as in *The framers of the Constitution were successful in achieving a balance of power.* Logical relations were primarily marked by the use of conjunctions. Consequential markers were especially significant in establishing the causes and conditions for the division of the government.

Elaboration, as this chapter has shown, was the most significant linguistic resource present in more successful essays and a distinguishing feature between the more and less successful essays. Elaboration of the macro-theme of the essay was particularly significant. The process of elaboration, through which writers can use different ways of presenting the same meanings, enables writers to organize their texts in ways that demonstrate the main points presented. Elaboration was realized through repetition, synonymy, and grammatical metaphor. Elaborating relationships were mainly present in introductions and conclusions to help writers present and reiterate their points. Teachers found the reiteration of ideas especially important, and they identified places in the essays where elaboration occurred as effective.

The linguistic features that inexperienced writers draw on when they write, as evidenced by the texts of ELLs, reveal their difficulty with aspects of the exposition genre. Learning to write in history depends on mastery of linguistic resources for the presentation of an organized and well-constructed essay. Those who "can't get it out right," as Jerry put it, must learn how to present their ideas in ways that are expected and appropriate in the discipline. Having no clear pattern of theme, as observed in Texts Three and Four, was not as successful as a constant theme or rheme to theme movement, as seen in the more successful essays. In addition, the inexperienced writers drew on patterns of spoken language to organize their essays, described as "writing in a speaking style." These choices did not help the writers to construct a more distanced and objective position expected of history writing. These writers' language choices created texts that, in teachers' views, are "subjective." In terms of elaboration, using simple repetition was not as successful as using synonymy and grammatical metaphor, present in the more successful essays. The way that students' ideas are presented and expressed can produce texts that do not conform to academic expectations. Based on the results presented in this chapter, Figure 4.2 shows the movement toward the highly valued in the exposition genre.

The analyses presented in this chapter illustrate some key linguistic features used by 8th-grade students in response to a prompt that elicited the exposition genre. The texts presented drew on the resources of theme, logical connections, and elaboration differently to organize and develop an exposition. The major differences between the more and less effective essays were in the way that the more effective essays used elaboration to develop and reiterate their ideas.

Making these language choices explicit to teachers can enable them to talk about both lexical and grammatical choices that construe academic registers. This should be done in order to show the potential in language to make meanings, building on what students bring to the task so that they can develop new ways of making meaning that are more academic. It is important to recognize that even though the writing task was the same, the way students responded to it differed. The way that language was used in these texts varied, as the analyses show.

Students need assistance in learning how to present historical information structured in ways that are appropriate for the academic task they are performing. Using the teachers' comments as a starting point, we saw that teachers have expectations in terms of how the historical information is to be presented and developed. While these expectations have to do with the topic or prompt, the expectations about how language is to be used in an expository writing task are clear. Teachers' expectations are realized *in* and *through* the language used by students to demonstrate their historical understanding. More explicit and linguistically oriented descriptions are necessary instead of just notions of what constitutes "strong writing." Teachers

**Theme**
No clear pattern of theme
Interpersonal themes that construct a subjective and hortatory style
Macro-theme that does not present or partially presents the writer's
position on the question

**Logical Connections**
Conjunctions of *addition* that organize text
Consequential conjunction *because* to show *cause*
Pervasive interactional style features

**Elaboration**
(through repetition)

Restating macro-theme

**Theme**
Use of theme as organizing device
Constant theme and rheme to theme movement
Macro-theme that presents the writer's position on the question
by answering it

**Logical Connections**
Conjunctions of *cause* and *condition*
Grammatical metaphor: Cause marked through verbs
More academic style, fewer interactional discourse features

**Elaboration**
(through repetition, synonymy, and grammatical metaphor)

Restating macro-theme
Moving from general to specific by giving examples
Renaming and restating points

**Figure 4.2** Movement toward the highly valued in exposition.

can learn how specific lexical and grammatical choices in the presentation of historical information constitute effective and successful texts. Providing explicit expectations for academic school history writing means giving students opportunities to talk about text and apprenticing them into the discipline of history.

The language resources of theme, logical connections, and elaboration can be the focus of pedagogy. Teachers can, for example, help students see how their thematic choices are creating the structuring of information in a text. In addition, students can consider the cohesive resources and logical connections they are employing to move from clause to clause that are contributing to the overall development of ideas. In particular, teachers can focus on the process of elaboration by helping students restate something already presented, include additional details, clarify points already discussed, explain, exemplify, and further describe. Synonymy, repetition, and grammatical metaphor are the grammatical processes through which elaboration is realized. Students can learn how to use synonyms to re-present their points, repeat certain language constructions and words effectively, and successfully use grammatical metaphor by rewording a meaning already introduced. Learning how to manipulate the language in new ways can take students from where they are now to where they can be, showing them the potential of language to expand and elaborate their ideas. Learning history means learning ways to express historical knowledge through language.

# Student Writing in History

## 11th Grade

What are the expectations for students' writing in school history? What are the language features that enable students to write an expository genre at the 11th-grade level in school history? In this chapter, I use three texts to illustrate some key linguistic features used by 11th-grade students in response to a prompt that elicited the exposition genre. These texts are representative of the corpus of 39 11th-grade essays analyzed and collected as part of an evaluation study conducted by the History Project. First, I present teachers' expectations for the expository writing task at the 11th-grade level, followed by the analyses of representative essays from the corpus. The analyses will show that the 8th- and the 11th-grade writing tasks elicited different kinds of writing patterns, so students drew on a different constellation of grammatical features to address each prompt. I demonstrate that writing an effective expository essay depends on deploying particular lexical and grammatical features that enable the presentation of a well-constructed essay.

## Teachers' Expectations for the Expository Writing Task

In this section, I draw on the discourse-based interviews to describe what teachers expected of students with each essay task at the 11th-grade level. The expository writing task was used in 11th-grade history classes as part of

*Knowing and Writing School History,* pages 89–123
Copyright © 2011 by Information Age Publishing

the evaluation study. The students were responding to a prompt that asked whether the sacrifices immigrants made and difficulties they endured were worth the new lives they created in the U.S. The prompt was an extended one that included the following parts: some background on immigration between 1870 and 1920, the question that students were supposed to address, and specific rhetorical features that students were expected to include (i.e., thesis, evidence, analysis, and conclusion). The language of the prompt provided students with some words that they could pick up and use, such as "living and working conditions." In the interviews, each 11th-grade teacher was asked a series of questions so that they could express their expectations.

Both 11th-grade teachers expected students to include information concerning the things immigrants left behind, such as family, language, customs, and food, among other things. In addition, they expected students to focus on the traveling conditions, especially the steerage conditions. They also expected them to include information on the kind of living conditions and working conditions that the immigrants experienced during that time period. Teachers also expected students to come to a conclusion as to whether they thought immigration was worth it for these people based on the kinds of political conditions and economic conditions that they left behind compared to what was possible in the U.S. According to the 11th-grade teachers, one of the key elements at this particular point in time was that in Europe there was absolutely no hope of economic advancement or any kind of social advancement, and in the U.S. there were many possibilities. Students would need to know what immigrants left behind and what they found in the U.S. and then provide an assessment of immigrants' decision.

As the analyses will show, the 8th- and the 11th-grade writing tasks elicited different kinds of writing patterns, so students drew on a different constellation of grammatical features to address each prompt. The 8th-grade prompt asked whether the framers of the Constitution were successful in achieving a balance of power or whether one branch had more powers than the other two. To answer that prompt, students drew on their knowledge of the Constitution to discuss the powers of each branch. They basically explained what those powers were and organized their essays with one paragraph dedicated to explaining each branch's powers. The 8th-grade writers used several language resources for defining the three branches with patterns of cause and condition to explain the division of government. More specifically, these resources included thematic choices through which the writers signaled the essay organizational structure and created a highly structured text organized around the three branches, with each branch serving as the point of departure of the body paragraphs; cohesive resources such as pronouns used to make links and establish relationships between elements of discourse; elaborating relationships to reiterate the main semantic notions present in the texts; and patterns of cause and condition used to establish logical relations to show the causes and conditions for the division of the government. These are enhanced through the use of additional resources at the 11th-grade level. This is partly due to the fact that this was a different prompt and topic. For the 11th-grade writing task, on the other hand, students had to describe the difficulties and sacrifices of immigrants by discussing their living and working conditions and then take a position on whether or not their move to the U.S. was worth it. Discussing immigrants' living and working conditions requires description, which in turn requires the use of *qualities*, such as *difficult* and *poor*. Therefore, resources for evaluation are particularly important for students not only to describe the living and working conditions of immigrants but also to make judgments about whether or not it was worth it for immigrants to come to the U.S. While students draw on causal patterns to present the causes of immigration, they also rely on concession to acknowledge alternative viewpoints that could be taken on this issue. The following section highlights these new and expanded language patterns at the 11th-grade level, comparing them to the 8th-grade corpus.

## Text Analysis and Results

Here I discuss two essays considered successful. As in the essays from the 8th-grade level, I look at thematic development and elaboration. The 11th-grade writing task was more complex than the 8th-grade writing task. The differing language patterns that students drew on to respond to the 11th-grade writing prompt show that even though both the 8th- and the 11th-grade writing prompts elicited patterns of exposition, the kinds of writing tasks were different. This demonstrates that teachers must be aware of the language demands placed on students by different writing tasks. Therefore, as we will see in the analyses, students draw on a different constellation of grammatical features to address the prompt.

The topic for the 11th grade asked writers to make judgments about whether or not it was worth it for immigrants to come to the U.S. This requires concession and contrast, two very important resources that students drew on to respond to the prompt. Writers also needed to describe the living and working conditions of immigrants to support their position. To do so, they needed to draw on resources for evaluation and description, which helped students to elaborate. And since writers were expected to describe the living and working conditions of immigrants, the analyses also focus on resources for description, especially relational processes (of *being*) such as *to be*, used to describe, classify, name, and evaluate. Therefore, the analyses focus on concession and contrast as logical connections as well as evaluative meanings and their expression through *being* processes. These resources are explained and exemplified in the contexts of the analyses. As we will see in this chapter, 11th-grade students draw on resources of theme to organize their essays, but for this topic, the rheme (where new information is built up) enables the presentation of what is being argued. In addition, in contrast to the 8th-grade essays, the 11th-grade writers used other, more sophisticated grammatical resources to elaborate. First, I present the analyses of Texts Five and Six, the essays considered successful. These essays are representative of the 11th-grade corpus that was analyzed, and they exemplify the full range of features used in other essays that were considered successful. They are also important because they show different approaches to the writing task but represent the main ways that students from the corpus responded to the prompt. The first essay was written by a native English speaker, while the second essay was written by a mainstreamed ELL.

___

*Example of Successful Essays: An English Speaker and an English Language Learner*

---

### TEXT FIVE

The immigrants coming from Eastern and Southern Europe endured many difficulties and made many sacrifices, all to begin a new life in the United States. These immigrants came to America to forget their old ways in their home countries. Their experiences were painful, but their effort and sacrifices they made were well worth the new life they would soon begin in America.

To make it here, in America, the immigrants would have to work. The working conditions here were rough and most of the time unfair. Some worked in mines, and others in factories. They were both very dangerous, as they were no safety supplies in either one. Children worked in the mines, some at age 10, and some older. These conditions were not a place for children to be. After all their hard work, the immigrants received very low pay. Most workers went on strike because of their unfair pay, but extra hard work, and when they did, the police interfered. These working conditions were awful, but what they did to make it by here in America.

Not only were the working conditions rough, so were the living conditions. The immigrant neighborhoods were poor and dirty, and very crowded. In one apartment, up to 10 people would live in it. Their homes were very cold and unheated. They were packed with blankets and people.

There was very little food, and most got sick. Most people would starve to death or die from a cold. These living conditions were outrageous, but was worth the freedom.

The immigrants were welcomed rudely and were discriminated. They weren't greeted kindly. This made the immigrants feel uncomfortable. Americans treated the immigrants like they were aliens, which was why they received unfair pay and horrible home life. The immigrants were not comfortable living here because they weren't greeted with kindness.

Even though the European and Asian immigrants made all these sacrifices and changes, their trip was worth the personal freedom they received here, and never got in their home countries. Their trip to America was worth their new lives.

The writer of Text Five has structured the essay in a way that is highly valued in expository writing. The writer begins with an introduction that clearly addresses the prompt. The introduction ends with a thesis that answers the question posed in the writing prompt, following the expectations for this type of writing. The essay proceeds to support the writer's position by providing historical information on the working and living conditions of immigrants, addressing the expectation presented in the prompt. Table 5.1 presents the thematic analysis of Text Five.

The thematic choices of Text Five show effective organizing strategies for moving the essay forward, while the rheme is functional for the accumulation of information that supports the development of the essay. The theme choices move between concrete and abstract participants as the writer moves from describing the conditions to evaluating them. In the rheme, the evaluation of the working and living conditions is presented and developed or the writer's perspective on the topic is presented. For example, in paragraph two, when the writer wants to provide an explanation about where the immigrants worked, he chooses concrete participants as themes, as in *Some* [*immigrants*] (clause 7), *others* (clause 8), and *children* (clause 11). Then new information about where immigrants worked is presented in the rheme. However, when the writer presents evaluation in the rheme, the thematic choices have to do with *conditions*, as in *The working conditions* (clause 6), *these conditions* (clause 12), and *These working conditions* (clause 17), and the rhemes give the assessment of these (*rough, unfair*). As in the successful 8th-grade examples, the successful 11th-grade essays use a constant thematic pattern and rheme to theme movement resources to move the essay forward.

**TABLE 5.1 Thematic Analysis of Text Five**

| Clause # | Interpersonal | Textual | Topical | Rheme |
|---|---|---|---|---|
| | | | **Theme** | |
| 1. | | | **The immigrants coming from Eastern and Southern Europe** | endured many difficulties and made many sacrifices, all to begin a new life in the United States. |
| 2. | | | **These immigrants** | came to America to forget their old ways in their home countries. |
| 3. | | | **Their experiences** | were painful |
| 4. | | but | **their effort and sacrifices they made** | were well worth the new life they would soon begin in America |
| 5. | | | **To make it here, in America,** | the immigrants would have to work. |
| 6. | | | **The working conditions here** | were rough and most of the time unfair. |
| 7. | | | **Some [immigrants]** | worked in mines, |
| 8. | | and | **others** | [worked] in factories |
| 9. | | | **They** | were both very dangerous, |
| 10. | | as | **there** | were no safety supplies in either one. |
| 11. | | | **Children** | worked in the mines, some at age 10, and some older. |
| 12. | | | **These conditions** | were not a place for children to be. |
| 13. | | | **After all their hard work,** | the immigrants received very low pay. |
| 14. | | | **Most workers** | went on strike because of their unfair pay, but extra hard work, |
| 15. | | and when | **they** | did, |
| 16. | | | **the police** | interfered. |
| 17. | | | **These working conditions** | were awful, |
| 18. | | but | **[it was] what they** | did to make it by here in America. |

| | | | |
|---|---|---|---|
| 19. | Not only | were | the working conditions rough |
| 20. | so | were | the living conditions [rough]. |
| 21. | | The immigrant neighborhoods | were poor and dirty, and very crowded. |
| 22. | | In one apartment, | up to 10 people would live in it |
| 23. | | Their homes | were very cold and unheated. |
| 24. | | They | were packed with blankets and people. |
| 25. | | There | was very little food, |
| 26. | and | most | got sick. |
| 27. | | Most people | would starve to death |
| 28. | or | [most people] | [would] die from a cold. |
| 29. | | These living conditions | were outrageous, |
| 30. | but | [these living conditions] | was worth the freedom. |
| 31. | | The immigrants | were welcomed rudely and were discriminated. |
| 32. | | They | weren't greeted kindly. |
| 33. | | This | made the immigrants feel uncomfortable. |
| 34. | | Americans | treated the immigrants like they were aliens, |
| 35. | | which | was why they received unfair pay and horrible home life. |
| 36. | | The immigrants | were not comfortable living here |
| 37. | because | they | weren't greeted with kindness. |
| 38. | Even though | the European and Asian immigrants | made all these sacrifices and changes, |
| 39. | | their trip | was worth the personal freedom they received here, and [the freedom they] never got in their home countries. |
| 40. | | Their trip to America | was worth their new lives. |

We saw in the 8th-grade sample that the macro-theme or thesis was an important feature. The macro-theme is also very significant for the 11th-grade essays. In Text Five, the writer's position on the topic is clearly presented in the macro-theme that gives a purpose for the essay. The essay prompt calls for the student to present a position on whether the sacrifices immigrants made and difficulties they endured were worth the new lives they created in the U.S. According to Maggie, the way this student addressed the prompt is particularly effective. Maggie states that the writer's thesis, presented in the introduction, presents "which side of the fence this one is on." The thematic information of the macro-theme serves as the orienter for the message that will be developed in the essay. The macro-theme of the essay is constructed in two clauses, which together form a clause complex. Clauses are linked together by logical-semantic relations to form clause complexes (Halliday & Matthiessen, 2004). While each clause has its thematic structure, each clause complex also has one thematic structure as a whole (Fries, 1995). Therefore, in Text Five, the first clause in the macro-theme, clause 3, *Their experiences were painful*, is thematic for the whole clause complex—it is the point of departure for the writer's position presented in the rheme (clause 4), *but their effort and sacrifices they made were well worth the new life they would soon begin in America,* which directly addresses the question in the prompt. The clause complex theme *Their experiences were painful* is not the focus of the writer's message but is an acknowledgement of immigrants' experiences, showing the writer's knowledge of the situation. This is the point of departure. The focus of the writer's message is in the rheme, which contains information directly relevant to the goals of the text. The writer acknowledges immigrants' experiences in the theme but moves on from there to present the focal information. We expect then that we would see historical information in the text that would support clause 4, something about why the effort and sacrifices immigrants made *were well worth the new life*. But this idea, as I present in the analysis, is never developed, just asserted.

### Evaluation and Elaboration as Development of Ideas

One of the major concerns of history teachers is students' lack of development of ideas in writing. Evaluation and elaboration are ways of accomplishing the development that history teachers often find missing in students' essays. Rather than asking students to "develop their ideas," teachers can help students see how such development can be accomplished linguistically through the grammatical and lexical processes used to construe evaluation and elaboration. In this section, I highlight ways that students used evaluation and elaboration to develop their ideas, presenting the value of rheme for the construction of text.

Unlike the essays from the 8th grade, evaluative meanings are particularly important for the 11th-grade writing task. Students were asked to describe the living and working conditions of immigrants and assess whether it was worth it for them to come to the U.S. To do so, students had to draw on evaluation resources. In systemic–functional linguistics (SFL), the system of *Appraisal* is concerned with evaluation. *Appraisal* is used as an umbrella term to cover evaluative uses of language and is a framework for investigating interpersonal meanings, or how attitudes are expressed in language (Coffin & Hewings, 2004; Martin & Rose, 2003). Figure 5.1 presents a summary of the Appraisal framework from Martin and Rose (2003). The framework includes resources for construing *Affect, Judgment,* and *Appreciation.*[1] For the purposes of this chapter, Appreciation is a useful construct since it is concerned with positive and negative assessments of objects, processes, and products rather than human behavior, the focus of resources of Affect and Judgment. The Appraisal system also includes resources for amplifying attitudes or for grading up or down in value. Graduation is a system of options for scaling meanings as force or focus. The grading of evaluative meanings is referred to in Figure 5.1 as *Graduation.* In clause 9, for instance, *very dangerous* represents scaling as force, where the quality *dangerous* is intensified by *very.* When qualities appear as nouns, such as in *danger,* scaling up in force is accomplished through quantification such as in *more danger.* Scaling up and down in force is the most useful appraisal resource for these essays. The framework also includes resources for *Engagement,* concerned with the source of attitudes, or where the evaluations are coming from. Engagement resources are used to include additional voices

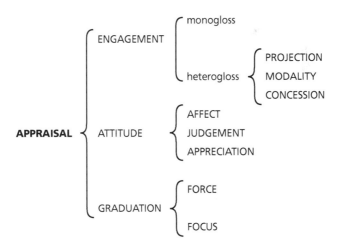

**Figure 5.1**   Appraisal framework adapted from Martin & Rose (2003).

into the discourse through projection, modality, and concession (Martin & Rose, 2003). The key distinction is one voice (*monogloss*) or different voices (*heterogloss*) (drawing on Bakhtin, 1981). As we will see, the 11th-grade writers bring in multiple voices (*heteroglossia*) as sources of evaluations. This is done through projection of others' words into the text via direct quotation or indirect reference; concession where different points of view are acknowledged; and modality, which expresses meanings that lie between *yes* and *no* and acknowledges alternative voices around a proposition or claim. These Engagement resources are all relevant for the 11th-grade analysis.

Appreciation resources include those that present both negative and positive value. The 11th-grade writers rely mostly on negative resources in evaluating the conditions, while they rely on positive resources to present their assertions. The resources of Appreciation enable the presentation of *qualities* in the form of positive and negative assessments. Appreciation meanings are present throughout Text Five. In paragraph one, for instance, *a new life*, a positive assessment, in clause 1 is contrasted with *their old ways*, a negative evaluation, in clause 2. We see this contrast present again in clause 3, where the writer talks about the experiences as *painful*; but in clause 5, the effort and sacrifices are presented as *worth something*. This writer uses the same pattern for showing evaluation throughout the essay by providing a contrast between the experiences as negative evaluation and the effort and sacrifices as positive. In presenting evaluation, the writer also relies on the use of the relational (or *being*) process *to be* for the presentation of qualities. In the macro-theme, the process *to be* is used in both clauses to present an evaluation. This *being* process is used to attribute a quality; it is called *attributive* in SFL. This *attributive process + quality* construction helps the writer to construct a point of view and argument as something objective, and the point is then reiterated in the rest of the essay. This same structure is found in other sentences in the essay, contributing to the construction of an authoritative stance. In paragraph two, we see the effective use of evaluation in clauses 6 and 9, where the qualities *rough, unfair*, and *dangerous* are presented through the attributive process *were*. These qualities express a negative evaluation. In clause 14, *Their unfair pay, but extra hard work* again mark the writer's assessment and develop the compare/contrast pattern with *unfair* and *extra hard*, using the comparative marker of contrast *but*. The third paragraph also presents evaluation. In clauses 21, 23, and 24, the attributive process *were* enables the presentation of negative evaluation in the rheme position in *poor and dirty, and very crowded; very cold and unheated;* and *packed with blankets and people. Very* in clauses 9, 13, 21, 23, and 25 is an example of a Graduation resource that scales the qualities up. Graduation resources are used in this text to intensify the negative Appreciation resources, such as in *well* in *well worth* (clause 4) and *extra* in *extra hard work* (clause 14), in addition to the clauses where *very* was used. In the fourth paragraph, where the writer describes other difficulties immigrants endured, evaluation of these experiences is presented through several evaluative words in rheme position, such as *rudely, discriminated, kindly, uncomfortable, unfair pay and horrible home life*, and *not comfortable*. The Appreciation resources enable the presentation of negative and positive evaluation, which helps the writer build a text that acknowledges the difficulties of immigrants' conditions but that also presents the trip as worth it. The writer of Text Five shows sophistication in the selection of evaluative meanings presented. Instead of repeating the same words, the writers use different words and wording to express similar meanings.

The accumulation of Appreciation resources in rheme position is presented in Table 5.2. Appreciation resources are in bold and italics, while Graduation resources are underlined.

**TABLE 5.2   Accumulation of Appreciation and Graduation Resources in Text Five**

| Clause # | Rheme |
|---|---|
| 1. | endured <u>many</u> *difficulties* and made <u>many</u> *sacrifices*, all to begin *a new life* in the United States. |
| 2. | came to America to forget *their old ways* in their home countries. |
| 3. | were *painful* |
| 4. | were <u>well</u> *worth the new life* they would soon begin in America |
| 5. | in America, the immigrants would have to work. |
| 6. | here were *rough* and most of the time *unfair.* |
| 7. | worked in mines, |
| 8. | [worked] in factories |
| 9. | were both <u>very</u> *dangerous,* |
| 10. | were *no safety supplies* in either one. |
| 11. | worked in the mines, some at age 10, and some older. |
| 12. | were *not a place for children to be.* |
| 13. | the immigrants received <u>very</u> *low pay.* |
| 14. | went on strike because of *their unfair pay,* but <u>extra</u> *hard work,* |
| 15. | did, |
| 16. | interfered. |
| 17. | were *awful,* |
| 18. | did to make it by here in America. |
| 19. | the working conditions *rough* |

*(continued)*

**TABLE 5.2 (continued)   Accumulation of Appreciation and Graduation Resources in Text Five**

| Clause # | Rheme |
|---|---|
| 20. | the living conditions [*rough*]. |
| 21. | were *poor and dirty, and* <u>very</u> *crowded.* |
| 22. | up to 10 people would live in it |
| 23. | were <u>very</u> *cold and unheated.* |
| 24. | were *packed with blankets and people.* |
| 25. | was <u>very</u> *little food,* |
| 26. | got sick. |
| 27. | would starve to death or die from a cold. |
| 28. | were *outrageous,* |
| 29. | was *worth* the *freedom.* |
| 30. | were welcomed *rudely* and were *discriminated.* |
| 31. | weren't greeted *kindly.* |
| 32. | made the immigrants feel *uncomfortable.* |
| 33. | treated the immigrants *like they were aliens,* |
| 34. | was why they received *unfair pay and horrible home life.* |
| 35. | were *not comfortable* living here |
| 36. | weren't greeted *with kindness.* |
| 37. | made all these *sacrifices and changes,* |
| 38. | was *worth* the *personal freedom* they received here, and [the freedom they] never got in their home countries. |
| 39. | was *worth* their *new lives.* |

In addition to the pattern in the use of Appreciation resources, the Engagement resource of *concession* is used in the more highly valued texts as a major organizing device. Concession is used in the texts to acknowledge opposite points of view. Concession is expressed primarily through the conjunction *but* in several clauses in this text. This conjunction construes concession or contrast, depending on how it is used in a particular context. In most of the clauses in Text Five, *but* is used to show concession, making a logical connection between the clauses that present the negative and the positive evaluation. These language choices combined enable the presentation of the writer's position. In clauses 3 and 4 in the first paragraph, for example, the writer is acknowledging that *Their experiences were painful,* but the concessive *but* counters this by indicating *their effort and sacrifices they made were well worth the new life they would soon begin in America.* Other patterns of concession are present in paragraph two. The marked theme in clause 13,

*After all their hard work*, shows concession, meaning "in spite of their hard work." Here we see both concession and Appreciation. This marked theme enables the evaluation to be expressed in the noun group *their hard work*, which picks up the ideas presented in clauses 7 through 12 and assesses the work done by immigrants, signaled by the word *hard*. The writer presents a negative evaluation in the rheme of the clause, *very low pay*, establishing a pattern of concession—although they worked hard (*their hard work*), they were paid poorly (*very low pay*).

This same pattern of concession is found in the final clauses of paragraphs two and three. We see an acknowledgement of the opposite point of view in clause 17, *These working conditions were awful*, but the concessive marker *but* in clause 18, *but what they did to make it by here in America*, shows the writer's position. This pattern appears again in clauses 29 and 30 of paragraph three. Clause 29 recognizes an opposite position, *These living conditions are outrageous*, but the concessive *but* introduces the writer's perspective, *but was worth the freedom*. This pattern occurs again in the conclusion of the essay. Clause 38 starts with the concessive marker *even though*, which acknowledges a different perspective: *Even though the European and Asian immigrants made all these sacrifices and changes*. Clause 39 presents the writer's point of view: *their trip was worth the personal freedom they received here and never got in their home countries*. This pattern of concession is very important for the topic of this essay, where students have to concede that things were difficult and yet make an argument that it was worth it for the immigrants to undergo the hardships.[2] This requires the contrasting and concession that pervade these essays. A pattern of concession also enables elaboration of meanings to be presented in other parts of the text, as we will see next.

Elaboration is a major textual move present in the successful essays. Elaboration is an especially significant pattern of meaning present in the most successful essays at both grade levels. As with the 8th-grade essays, elaboration of the macro-theme was a valued and distinguishing feature of the more successful 11th-grade essays. But while the 8th-grade essays relied primarily on repetition and synonymy to elaborate clauses, the essays from the 11th grade used other resources to elaborate. These resources included meronymy, collocation, and grammatical metaphor. The general sense of *meronymy* is "be a part of" (Halliday & Matthiessen, 2004), and here students use meronymy by selecting lexical items related to other items in part–whole or whole–part relationships. *Collocation* refers to the relationship between a sequence of words that often go together, or co-occur. The lexical items may not have any semantic relationship, but there is a direct association between them in their contexts of use (Halliday & Matthiessen,

2004). In the most successful essays, grammatical metaphor is used more often than in the 8th-grade texts. Elaboration was also enhanced through the addition of information in the elaborating clauses, as we will see in the following examples.

It is through elaboration that examples, clarifications, additional details, and explanations are provided. These are the "specifics" that Maggie described as being important aspects of Text Five. In discussing the second paragraph, for example, Maggie commented on how the student is "talking about the working conditions, that they were *unfair* conditions, that it was *dangerous*."[3] In addition, according to Maggie, the third paragraph is effective because it has "specifics, *no safety regulations, and children worked in mines.*" Maggie values this paragraph because it again presents "very specific things, *neighborhoods poor, dirty and very crowded, up to 10 people in a living space, cold and unheated, people starved to death because they didn't have very much food.*" This "presentation of specific things" is done through grammatical processes through which elaboration is accomplished. The role of elaboration in Text Five is presented in the following examples. It is not just the presence of elaboration that is important, but how elaboration is accomplished through the grammatical and lexical choices.

In the second paragraph, the nominal group *The working conditions* in clause 6 enables the writer to construct a clause that elaborates on the notion of *work* (introduced in clause 5) through grammatical metaphor, where the verb *work* is re-packaged as *the working conditions*, serving as the point of departure for the clause and enabling the forward movement of the essay with the presentation of the evaluation (*rough* and *unfair*) in rheme position. Clauses 7–12 elaborate on the negative assessment *rough*, explaining how the working conditions were *rough*, adding information about where immigrants worked, in *mines* and *factories*. Clauses 13–16 elaborate on the negative assessment *unfair*, presented in clause 6, by explaining how the working conditions were *unfair* because immigrants got low pay.

Several elaborating relationships are present in the third paragraph. The thematic choices in this paragraph present locations in *The immigrant neighborhoods, In one apartment, their homes*, and *they* [their homes]. The marked theme *In one apartment* is particularly significant because this thematic choice enables a constant pattern of locations to be presented in the theme. The elaborating relationship between these themes is accomplished through meronymy, or whole–part. The first location, *The immigrant neighborhoods*, represents the "whole," while *In one apartment, their homes*, and *they* represent "parts." Another elaborating relation occurs in clause 25, which introduces a problem of the living conditions, *little food*. This problem leads to another problem, presented in clause 26, *and most got sick*. This clause is elaborated in clauses 27 and 28, which clarify clauses 25 and 26. *Would starve to death* in clause 27 is a result of having *little food*, presented in clause 25, and *die from a cold* from clause 28 is a result of getting *sick*, presented in clause 26. These pairs of words are associated through collocation. This information in rheme position further develops the idea that the living conditions were *rough*, presented in clause 20.

In paragraph four, clause 34 elaborates clause 31. What is presented as *were discriminated* in clause 31 is reiterated as *Americans treated immigrants like they were aliens* in clause 34. Clause 35 elaborates on clause 34 by providing an explanation of the situation and identifying the reasoning for the rough working conditions, presented in *unfair pay*, and outrageous living conditions, presented in *horrible home life*. In other words, it was because *Americans treated immigrants like they were aliens* that immigrants *received unfair pay and horrible home life*. Clause 35, therefore, also makes a logical connection to clause 34, signaled by *why*. The non-restrictive clause introduced by the relative pronoun *which, which was why they received unfair pay and horrible home life*, refers backward to the rheme of clause 34 and elaborates on the meanings presented there.

### Hyper-themes: Essay Organization Revealed

While clause themes help the writer organize information and provide a framework for the interpretation of the clause, and macro-themes function as themes for the essay, a *hyper-theme* is the theme of the paragraph, giving an orientation to what is to come. Hyper-themes provide a framework for the paragraph. When hyper-themes are used effectively, as we will see in Text Five, they contribute to the overall organizational structure of the essay, helping the writer provide a framework for the ideas and helping the reader to follow what is being presented and developed. Hyper-themes appear in 11th-grade essays as major organizing devices for the paragraph. Successful essays from the 11th-grade corpus use hyper-themes to give an orientation to what was presented in each body paragraph. We see in the next examples how Appreciation resources, concession, and elaboration are used within the hyper-themes and restatement of hyper-themes to create a very cohesive text.

The hyper-theme of paragraph two, for instance, is realized in two clauses (*To make it here, in America, the immigrants would have to work. The working conditions here were rough and most of the time unfair*) and gives an orientation to what will be developed in the paragraph, predicting the focus of the paragraph's idea. Paragraph two begins a discussion of immigrants' working conditions. The first clause of paragraph two is a bridge between the introduction and the body paragraph, with a consequential marker of purpose (*to make it here*) as the theme introducing the entire paragraph. The paragraph develops the message presented in the hyper-theme with examples of what those working conditions were. This hyper-theme is realized in two clauses, thus reinforcing the idea that the "topic sentence" of the paragraph does not necessarily need to be placed in the first position and can be more than one sentence, giving more prominence to the *function* rather than the *placement* of the paragraph's message.

The hyper-theme is reiterated in clauses 17 and 18. Even though the description of the working conditions in this paragraph is mostly negative, the conclusion the writer comes to in the final clauses of the paragraph presents a different interpretation, that the working conditions were *what they did to make it by here in America*. Clause 18 presents the situation as being almost inevitable, another underlying pattern used in this text. The thematic choice *these working conditions* takes the reader back to the theme of clause 6 and functions as a reference backward to the working conditions just described throughout the paragraph, with the demonstrative *these* making the connection. The negative evaluation appears in clause 17 and the positive assessment appears in clause 18. If we consider the thematic information of the entire clause complex, the theme *These working conditions were awful* presents the negative and the rheme *but what they did to make it by here in America* marks the positive, following the same structure of the macro-theme. Here, again, we see the use of the consequential marker of concession *but*. These two clauses, then, bring the entire paragraph back to the idea presented in the macro-theme, an expectation of the 11th-grade teachers. The demonstrative *these* in theme position links back to what has been said so that an evaluation can be presented.

The hyper-theme of the third paragraph, *Not only were the working conditions rough, so were the living conditions*, functions as a transition, linking the clause back to what was already presented in paragraph two (*the working conditions*) and foregrounding what is going to be the focus of the current paragraph, *the living conditions* of immigrants. The hyper-theme is a comparative structure that enables the presentation of a comparison, and the evaluative word *rough*, which appeared in clause 6, is repeated to show the negative assessment. The hyper-theme is reiterated in clauses 29 and 30, presenting the "conclusion" the writer comes to at the end of the paragraph. Maggie finds these final clauses particularly effective because, like in the previous paragraph, they refer back to the thesis. In clause 28, the thematic choice *these living conditions* takes the reader back to the rheme of clause 20 and functions as a reference backward to the living conditions just described throughout the paragraph, with the demonstrative *these* again making the connection. As in clauses 17 and 18, the negative evaluation (*were outrageous*) appears in clause 28 and the positive assessment (*was worth the freedom*) appears in clause 29. If we consider the thematic information of the entire clause complex, the theme *These living conditions were outrageous* presents the negative and the rheme *but was worth the freedom* marks the positive, following the same structure of clauses 17 and 18 as well as the macro-theme. The demonstrative *these* in theme position again links back to what has been said so that an evaluation can be presented. The rheme is presenting new information that has not been presented in the essay, that immigrants also gained *freedom*. This is the first reference to *freedom* in the essay, but this semantic notion is mentioned again in the conclusion of the essay as something that immigrants received.

As in paragraph two, the hyper-theme of the fourth paragraph is realized in two clauses (*The immigrants were welcomed rudely and were discriminated. They weren't greeted kindly*) predicting what is to come in the paragraph, a focus on the treatment of immigrants when they arrived in the U.S. This paragraph serves to provide further evidence for the experiences of immigrants. The hyper-theme is reiterated in clauses 35 and 36. The consequential marker *because* indicates the cause, *they weren't greeted with kindness*, making a logical connection with the previous clause and justifying the writer's position that *The immigrants were not comfortable living here*. Again we see negative evaluation being presented in rheme position in both clauses, in *not comfortable* and *weren't greeted with kindness*.

Conclusions at this level are expected to summarize main points, to underscore important positions, and to remind readers of previous assertions. The concluding paragraph, according to Maggie, shows that immigrants "made all these sacrifices and changes and really they still thought *Their trip to America was worth their new lives*." Clauses 37 and 38 elaborate the macro-theme by restating it, reinforcing the writer's position. The consequential marker *even though* signals a concession in which clause 37 presents a negative evaluation in the rheme *made all these sacrifices and changes*, and clause 38 presents the positive assessment, *was worth the personal freedom they received here and never got in their home countries*. The last clause, clause 39, *Their trip to America was worth their new lives*, restates the main idea of the essay. This clause also elaborates the rheme of the macro-theme through repetition of *worth* and *new lives*. Maggie found that "this essay was really well organized. The paragraphs stayed with a main thought and in the conclusion, it came back to the prompt." As Maggie puts it, "we have this consistency in this particular essay and I was very pleased to see that." The consistency Maggie talks about is a combination of the linguistic resources of theme, concession, evaluation, cohesive resources, and elaboration. However, the historical information presented in the conclusion again might lead the reader to conclude that the sacrifices and efforts of immigrants were not worth the new lives they created. The position presented in the macro-theme, that *their effort and sacrifices they made were well worth the new life they would soon begin in America,* is never fully supported by the historical information on the conditions and experiences of immigrants, which supports a different position, namely, that the conditions and experiences were *not* worth the new life in the U.S. This is certainly a weakness of this essay, but one that Maggie did not highlight, since the essay is "consistent" in the presentation of historical information on the working and living conditions of immigrants.

The general patterns found in the successful essays of the 11th-grade corpus constitute hyper-themes that are presented at the beginning of a paragraph and reiterated at the end, both following a concessive pattern that enables writers to recognize an opposing viewpoint and at the same time presenting the writer's own viewpoint. As previously mentioned, the reiteration of the hyper-themes presented in paragraphs two and three of Text Five follows a concessive pattern in which the concessive marker *but* enables the acknowledgement of an opposite point of view with a negative evaluation and the presentation of the writer's view with a positive assessment. This pattern of concession is also present in the macro-theme and the restatement of the macro-theme in the concluding paragraph, clauses 38 and 39. This pattern of concession and presentation of evaluation makes this text very cohesive.

The hyper-themes used in Text Five provide an organizational framework for each paragraph. They are used effectively to present an overall organizational structure of the essay, helping the writer provide a framework for the ideas and helping the reader to follow what is being presented and developed. Unlike the 8th-grade essays, 11th grade essays use hyper-themes effectively, contributing to the overall success of the essays.

The reiteration of hyper-themes in the final clauses of the paragraph was an effective way of elaborating on the ideas. Figure 5.2 presents the macro-theme, the hyper-theme of each paragraph, and the elaboration presented in each paragraph.

The following example, Text Six, shows another approach to this writing task. To present their knowledge of this topic, students needed to be able to describe the working and living conditions of immigrants and assess whether the difficulties immigrants faced were worth the new lives they gained in the United States. This topic requires judgment and evaluation through Appreciation resources that build evaluation and present

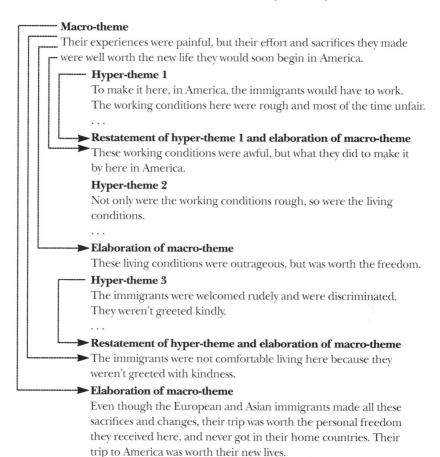

**Macro-theme**
Their experiences were painful, but their effort and sacrifices they made were well worth the new life they would soon begin in America.

**Hyper-theme 1**
To make it here, in America, the immigrants would have to work. The working conditions here were rough and most of the time unfair.
. . .

**Restatement of hyper-theme 1 and elaboration of macro-theme**
These working conditions were awful, but what they did to make it by here in America.

**Hyper-theme 2**
Not only were the working conditions rough, so were the living conditions.
. . .

**Elaboration of macro-theme**
These living conditions were outrageous, but was worth the freedom.

**Hyper-theme 3**
The immigrants were welcomed rudely and were discriminated. They weren't greeted kindly.
. . .

**Restatement of hyper-theme and elaboration of macro-theme**
The immigrants were not comfortable living here because they weren't greeted with kindness.

**Elaboration of macro-theme**
Even though the European and Asian immigrants made all these sacrifices and changes, their trip was worth the personal freedom they received here, and never got in their home countries. Their trip to America was worth their new lives.

**Figure 5.2** Macro-theme, hyper-themes, and elaboration.

the writer's perspective in rheme position. The resources of elaboration, through which ideas can be expanded and developed, are particularly relevant for the 11th-grade level. Concession and contrast were also major organizing devices, since the essay topic required students to concede that things were difficult and yet make an argument that coming to the United States was worth the difficulty for the immigrants. Text Six was written by a mainstreamed ELL and was assessed as a successful essay. According to Maggie, this student shows historical understanding about immigrants. I present Maggie's assessment of the essay in the context of the linguistic analysis.

---

**TEXT SIX**

Many immigrants have traveled to the United States for years. Between 1870 and 1920 millions of immigrants came from Europe and Asia. Immigrants came to the U.S., because they were in search for a better and new life.

Immigrants traveled to the U.S. on boats. To many the trip was very difficult, because most of the time they could not afford it. For those who could afford it, had a pretty good trip, but the rest had horrible conditions that they had to endure on their journey here. Once an immigrant arrived in the U.S. they had to find jobs immediately, because that was the only way they could survive, so they took any job that was offered.

Most immigrants had really low-paying jobs that could not support the whole family, so everyone had to work. Immigrants mostly worked in the factories where the conditions were terrible. They worked all day with unsafe surroundings, and got low pay. Some would also die from the hazardous jobs they had to do.

American citizens could see that many foreigners were moving in, and most felt that they were taking up all the jobs that belonged to them. Racism became an issue, because white men or some believed that the immigrants should not be able to have jobs that rightfully belonged to them. Many hate crimes were involved and several immigrants had to live with the racism, even old immigrants taunted new ones, because they knew that they might take over.

The overall experience for an immigrant was a pretty tough one. Many used their last penny in hopes of making it big in the U.S. They also lived in conditions that were incredibly bad, and their jobs basically killed them. Many immigrants fled a life of poverty and came to the U.S. and still lived in poverty. For most their life did not change, but for those who came from nothing and became something, the journey was well worth it. They worked hard, well all immigrants did, but those who were lucky got what they came for, which was a better, new and improved life. Although the dream did not come true for all immigrants, it definitely broadened their minds as well as others. I'm glad to say that my parents came here for a better life, because that gave me a chance to experience all the opportunities America has to offer.

---

Table 5.3 presents the thematic analysis of Text Six, followed by the linguistic analysis.

Text Six, according to Maggie, like other successful essays from the 11th-grade corpus, is a strong essay because it is "organized [and] has back-up facts and evidence." Clauses 3 and 4 are the macro-theme or thesis of the essay and indicate *why* immigrants came, realized by the consequential

**TABLE 5.3  Thematic Analysis of Text Six**

| Clause # | Theme | | | Rheme |
|---|---|---|---|---|
| | Interpersonal | Textual | Topical | |
| 1. | | | **Many immigrants** | have traveled to the United States for years. |
| 2. | | | **Between 1870 and 1920** | millions of immigrants came from Europe and Asia. |
| 3. | | | **Immigrants** | came to the U.S., |
| 4. | | because | they | were in search for a better and new life. |
| 5. | | | **Immigrants** | traveled to the U.S. on boats. |
| 6. | | | **To many** | the trip was very difficult, |
| 7. | | because | most of the time | they could not afford it. |
| 8. | | but | **For those who could afford it,** | had a pretty good trip |
| 9. | | | the rest | had horrible conditions that they had to endure on their journey here. |
| 10. | | Once | an immigrant | arrived in the U.S. |
| 11. | | | they | had to find jobs immediately, |
| 12. | | because | that | was the only way they could survive, |
| 13. | | so | they | took any job that was offered. |
| 14. | | | **Most immigrants** | had really low-paying jobs that could not support the whole family, |
| 15. | | so | everyone | had to work. |
| 16. | | | **Immigrants** | mostly worked in the factories |
| 17. | | | **where [factories]** | the conditions were terrible. |
| 18. | | | **They** | worked all day with unsafe surroundings, |
| 19. | | and | [they] | got low pay. |
| 20. | | | **Some** | would also die from the hazardous jobs they had to do. |
| 21. | | | **American citizens** | could see that many foreigners were moving in, |

*(continued)*

**TABLE 5.3 (continued)  Thematic Analysis of Text Six**

| Clause # | Interpersonal | Textual | Theme Topical | Rheme |
|---|---|---|---|---|
| 22. | | and | most | felt |
| 23. | | that | they | were taking up all the jobs that belonged to them. |
| 24. | | | Racism | became an issue, |
| 25. | | because | white men or some | believed |
| 26. | | that | the immigrants | should not be able to have jobs that rightfully belonged to them. |
| 27. | | | Many hate crimes | were involved |
| 28. | | and | several immigrants | had to live with the racism, |
| 29. | | | even old immigrants | taunted new ones, |
| 30. | | because | they | knew |
| 31. | | that | they | might take over. |
| 32. | | | The overall experience for an immigrant | was a pretty tough one. |
| 33. | | | Many | used their last penny in hopes of making it big in the U.S.. |
| 34. | | | They | also lived in conditions that were incredibly bad, |

| | | | |
|---|---|---|---|
| 35. | | their jobs | basically killed them. |
| 36. | and | Many immigrants | fled a life of poverty |
| 37. | and | | came to the U.S. |
| 38. | and | | still lived in poverty. |
| 39. | | For most | their life did not change, |
| 40. | but | for those who came from nothing and became something, | the journey was well worth it. |
| 41. | | They | worked hard, |
| 42. | well | all immigrants | did, |
| 43. | but | those who were lucky | got what they came for, |
| 44. | | which [what they came for] | was a better, new and improved life. |
| 45. | Although | the dream | did not come true for all immigrants, |
| 46. | | it | definitely broadened their minds as well as others. |
| 47. | I'm glad to say that | my parents | came here for a better life, |
| 48. | because | that | gave me a chance to experience all the opportunities America has to offer. |

marker of cause *because* in clause 4. Unlike Text Five, however, the macro-theme does not present the writer's perspective as to whether or not it was worth it for immigrants to move to the U.S. The essay was considered strong primarily because it has specific details, a major feature of the successful essays, which was attained through elaboration, as the analysis shows.

As in Text Five, there are positive Appreciation resources presented in rheme position in several clauses. In the rheme of clause 4, a positive assessment is used to describe the reason of immigrants' move, *a better and new life*. Paragraph two, as Maggie stated, presents information "about the difficulty of the trip and the reasons [for making it]." This paragraph contains several evaluative meanings signaled by Appreciation resources, both negative and positive, in several clauses. The text presents mostly negative evaluation, with some positive evaluative meanings presented when the writer talks about those for whom the trip was worth the difficulty. The text also uses Graduation resources, which present options for scaling meanings as force. In clause 4, for instance, *very difficult* represents scaling as force, where the quality *difficult* is intensified by *very*. Appreciation and Graduation resources in Text Six are presented in Table 5.4. Appreciation resources are in bold and italics and Graduation resources are underlined.

The writer of Text Six, unlike the writer of Text Five, qualifies several of the statements and presents the position that the trip was worth it for some but not for all immigrants. While Text Five uses concession to put forth an opposing viewpoint, Text Six uses qualifiers, such as *many* and *some*, in theme position to establish that the trip was not worth it for all immigrants. For instance, the theme of clause 8, *for those who could afford it*, is used to introduce a contrast between the information presented in the rheme of clause 6 and the rheme of clause 8, *had a pretty good trip*, a positive evaluation. The contrast, then, is established between those who could afford the trip and those who could not. This expression that the trip was not worth it for all immigrants is reiterated in the last paragraph through the thematic choices *many* (clause 33) and *for most* (clause 39).

Engagement resources are used in this text to bring outside voices into the texts. Projection, modality, and concession are the three Engagement resources that the writer of Text Six relies on. Concession is also used in this text to present opposing points of view, but it is used less often than in Text Five. The writer uses the resources of projection and modality more often to introduce additional voices into the text. While Text Five used concession to bring in opposing views and present the writer's own view, Text Six uses projection to bring in outside voices. In clause 9, the consequential marker *but* indicates concession alongside the modality constructing ne-

**TABLE 5.4  Accumulation of Appreciation and Graduation Resources in Text Six**

| Clause # | Rheme |
|---|---|
| 4 | were in search for *a better and new life.* |
| 6 | the trip was <u>very</u> *difficult,* |
| 8 | had *a* <u>pretty</u> *good trip* |
| 9 | had *horrible conditions* that they had to *endure* on their journey here. |
| 12 | was the only way they could *survive,* |
| 14 | had <u>really</u> *low-paying jobs* that could not support the whole family, |
| 17 | the conditions were *terrible.* |
| 18 | worked all day with *unsafe surroundings,* |
| 19 | got *low pay.* |
| 20 | would also *die from the hazardous jobs* they had to do. |
| 24 | became *an issue,* |
| 26 | should not be able to have jobs that *rightfully belonged* to them. |
| 28 | had to live with the *racism,* |
| 29 | *taunted* new ones, |
| 31 | might *take over.* |
| 32 | was *a* <u>pretty</u> *tough one.* |
| 33 | used their last penny in hopes of *making it big* in the U.S.. |
| 34 | also lived in *conditions that were* <u>incredibly</u> *bad,* |
| 35 | basically *killed* them. |
| 36 | fled *a life of poverty* |
| 37 | came to the U.S. |
| 38 | still *lived in poverty.* |
| 39 | their *life did not change,* |
| 40 | the journey was <u>well</u> *worth it.* |
| 41 | worked *hard,* |
| 44 | was *a better, new and improved life.* |
| 45 | *did not come true* for <u>all</u> immigrants, |
| 46 | *definitely broadened their minds* as well as others. |
| 47 | came here for *a better life,* |
| 48 | gave me a chance to experience all the *opportunities* America has to offer. |

cessity in *had to*, as well as the verb *endure*, which denotes a hardship. The consequential marker of concession *but* is used again in clause 40 to create a contrast between immigrants whose lives did not change and those whose lives changed, with the rheme of clause 40, *the journey was well worth it*, presenting a contrast with *their life did not change*, the rheme of clause 39. The concessive marker *Although* in clause 45 recognizes the perspective that *the dream did not come true for all immigrants*, but adds the writer's point of view, *it definitely broadened their minds as well as others.*

The Engagement resource of modality indicating necessity and obligation is used in this text in several clauses to reiterate the inevitability of this situation for immigrants, also present in Text Five. In Text Six, this modality is seen in clause 11, *had to find jobs immediately*; clause 15, *everyone had to work*; clause 20, *the hazardous jobs they had to do*; and clause 28, *had to live with the racism.* This modality of necessity expressed in *had to* indicates inevitable situations. The modality is further supported by the use of *the only way* in the rheme of clause 12, *was the only way they could survive*, which presents the cause as being inevitable.

Projection resources are used to "implicitly or explicitly attribute discourse to speaker/writers other than the author" (Martin, 2004, p. 331). Projection is used to acknowledge alternative sources, increasing the range of voices in the text (Martin, 2004). In the 11th-grade corpus, projection brings in the voices of others to present their perspectives. In Text Six, projection is used primarily in paragraph four, where we see a shift in the focus of the information in clause 21, with the thematic choice *American citizens.* This paragraph, then, focuses on how immigrants were perceived and received and the problems that surfaced in consequence, seen in the thematic choices *Racism* (clause 24) and *Many hate crimes* (clause 27). In this paragraph, projection enables the writer to bring in outside voices to express American citizens' *feelings* and *beliefs.* Projection through the mental processes *felt* (clause 22) and *believed* (clause 25) enables the presentation of American citizens' views to show how the problems developed. Text Six uses projection to bring in outside voices, unlike Text Five, which used concession to highlight opposing views and display the writer's own view. Projection through the mental process *knew* shows a strong view of *old immigrants.*

Elaboration is also very relevant for the development of the ideas presented in Text Six, accomplished through a number of different grammatical processes. Elaboration in Text Six is done primarily through repetition, synonymy, and grammatical metaphor. In clause 5, for instance, *traveled to the U.S.* is re-packaged through grammatical metaphor as *their trip* in clause 6. Then in clause 9, the further repacking as *their journey* enables the writer to elaborate on *their trip.* Clause 13 introduces *jobs* in the notion of *any job*, elaborated in several clauses, where jobs are described as *low-paying* (clause 14). Clauses 25–26 elaborate on clauses 22–23, with the rewording of what was presented as a *feeling* in clause 23 as a *belief* in clause 26, which is presented as a cause for the development of racism. The consequence of racism, then, is presented as the point of departure of clause 27, *many hate crimes*.

*Used their last penny* in the rheme of clause 33 elaborates on *they could not afford it*, presented in clause 7. Clause 35 elaborates on clause 20; more specifically, the process *killed* in rheme position in clause 35 reiterates *would also die from* in the rheme of clause 20. Clauses 36, 37, and 38 are used to make a comparison between what immigrants *fled* and what they *lived* in the U.S. The idea of *poverty* has already been brought up semantically in what immigrants left, presented in *could not afford it* (clause 7) and *used their last penny* (clause 33), as well as what they found in the U.S.: *low-paying jobs* (clause 14) and *low-pay* (clause 19).

As we saw from the examples, 11th-grade writers made judgments about whether or not it was worth it for immigrants to come to the U.S. Two very important resources that students drew on to respond to the prompt were concession and contrast. Writers described the living and working conditions of immigrants to support their position, drawing on resources for evaluation and description that helped students to elaborate. Resources for description, especially relational processes (of *being*) such as *to be*, were used to describe, classify, name, and evaluate. Concession and contrast as logical connections and the expression of evaluative meanings as Appreciation resources through *being* processes were particularly relevant. These resources were explained and exemplified in the contexts of the analyses. The 11th-grade writers drew on resources of theme to organize their essays, but for this topic, the rheme, where new information is built up, enabled the presentation of what was argued. In addition, in contrast to the 8th-grade essays, the 11th-grade writers used other, more sophisticated grammatical resources to elaborate. The successful essays are important because they show different approaches to the writing task, representing the main ways that students from the corpus responded to the prompt. The additional resources used in the 11th-grade corpus are briefly summarized in Figure 5.3.

Figure 5.3 includes hyper-themes that provide a framework for each paragraph, particularly important at the 11th-grade level for the organization and structuring of the information. Elaboration is a very significant feature in the 11th-grade corpus, achieved through meronymy, collocation, and grammatical metaphor. Elaboration of the macro-theme and hyper-themes is particularly relevant at the 11th-grade level. Evaluation resources are important ways for describing and judging. Attributive processes are used to construe negative and positive evaluation, presented through Appreciation resources. Engagement is used to bring additional voices into the

---

**Theme**

Use of theme as organizing device

Rheme accumulates information that supports the development of the essay

Marked themes that help structure the essay

Hyper-themes that provide a framework for each paragraph

**Logical Connections**

Conjunctions of *concession*

**Elaboration**

through grammatical metaphor, meronymy, and collocation

Restating macro-theme and hyper-themes

Moving from general to specific by giving examples

Renaming and restating points

Adding more detail or further specifying

**Evaluation**

*Resources for Appreciation*

Attributive processes that construct descriptions and judgments

Negative and positive assessments

*Resources for Engagement*

**Projection** through mental processes to bring others' words into the text via direct quotation or indirect reference

**Concession** through conjunctions (e.g., *but, even though, although*) to acknowledge different points of view

**Modality** that expresses necessity and obligation (*have/had to*) to reiterate the inevitability of the situation for immigrants and to acknowledge alternative voices around a proposition or claim

*Resources for Graduation*

Grading up and down through adverbs and other resources for intensifying evaluation

---

**Figure 5.3** Additional language resources used at the 11th-grade level.

discourse through projection, modality, and concession. To demonstrate the value of these language features, we can contrast the more successful essays with the way a less successful writer developed his essay.

---

## Example of an Essay in Need of Improvement

While Texts Five and Six were considered effective essays, Text Seven was assessed by Peter as in need of improvement. In discussing this essay, I contrast it with the successful essays and present the areas where the essay could be improved, explaining what teachers could do to help this student expand on and develop his ideas.

---

**TEXT SEVEN**

In the late 1800s there was a large increase in the number of new immigrants. Many left their home in search of new and better life. Once in America, however, they were met with everything but welcoming arms. These new people had to make lots of sacrifices as well as constant discrimination. All those sacrifices where not made up for by the new life that they were sure they were able to get jobs and support themselves. But the work was hard and paid little. They constantly were made aware of their differences and by most nativists were seen as inferior and lower than the lowest class. Even to this day the newer immigrant groups are not given the respect they deserve.

The number of immigrants that actually made lives for themselves wasn't that large. For a long time most new Americans were making up the lowest class of society that were forced to things that most Americans wouldn't take as work these tasks were either too dangerous or too hazardous.

---

Table 5.5 presents the thematic analysis of Text Seven.

This essay lacks the organizational structure present in Texts Five and Six. With only two paragraphs, the essay does not develop any of the ideas presented by means of elaboration and evaluation, as we saw in Texts Five and Six. As Peter said, there is "only this rather large paragraph" where the student "kind of just throws everything in." According to Peter, "There's really no introduction and it's not really clear that if they're [immigrants] searching for a new and better life, did they find it? Where's your thesis statement?" Peter finds that this writer should have provided a thesis statement in the introduction, where a position on the topic would have been presented. According to Peter, there is one such attempt in *Many left their home in search for a new and better life. These new people had to make lots of sacrifices as well as constant discrimination.* Peter says that "the student mentions that, which most of the other papers don't." But Peter mentions that in *All those sacrifices were not made up for by the new life that they were sure they were able to get jobs and support themselves,* "you kind of lose what they are saying here, so this essay doesn't really seem to go anywhere." The essay "does not directly answer the question posed in the prompt," as Peter says.

The first paragraph contains several clauses that could be further developed. As Peter suggested, the ideas presented in this paragraph could be better developed and organized. For instance, clause 2, *Many left their home in search of new and better life,* marks a cause for why immigrants left, but, as Peter said, the writer does not present whether or not they found this better

**TABLE 5.5  Thematic Analysis of Text Seven**

| Clause # | Textual | Topical | Rheme |
|---|---|---|---|
| | | **Theme** | |
| 1. | | **In the late 1800s** | there was a large increase in the number of new immigrants. |
| 2. | | **Many** | left their home in search of new and better life. |
| 3. | | **Once in America,** | however, they were met with everything but welcoming arms. |
| 4. | | **These new people** | had to make lots of sacrifices as well as constant discrimination. |
| 5. | | **All those sacrifices** | were not made up for by the new life that they were sure they were able to get jobs and support themselves. |
| 6. | **But** | **the work** | was hard |
| 7. | **and** | **[the work]** | paid little. |
| 8. | | **They** | constantly were made aware of their differences |
| 9. | **and** | **by most nativists** | were seen as inferior and lower than the lowest class. |
| 10. | | **Even to this day** | the newer immigrant groups are not given the respect they deserve. |
| 11. | | **The number of immigrants that actually made lives for themselves** | wasn't that large. |
| 12. | | **For a long time** | most new Americans were making up the lowest class of society that were forced to things that most Americans wouldn't take as work |
| 13. | | **these tasks** | were either too dangerous or too hazardous. |

new life or whether or not it was worth it for them to leave their countries. Clause 3 presents the difficulty that immigrants faced in rheme position, expressed in *however, they were met with everything but welcoming arms*. But here the writer does not state what those conditions were. The writer could have expanded this clause by providing examples of those not so "welcoming arms." This would be a good opportunity for the writer to use evaluation to describe the conditions. The theme of clause 4, *these new people*, refers back to *new immigrants* in clause 1, and then the rheme goes back to the essay prompt in *had to make lots of sacrifices. Constant discrimination* is linked to lots of sacrifices by an additive marker *as well as*, but this additive marker is not enough to make an effective link. The writer may perhaps be trying to say that new immigrants *suffered* or *had to deal* with *constant discrimination* and not that they *had to make [. . .] constant discrimination*. This *constant discrimination* was a problem for immigrants, and the writer stops there in his description, when he could have expanded this and gone on to describe what immigrants faced, like the writer of Text Five did in the third paragraph of the essay. Clause 5 is an attempt to present a position on the question, that the *sacrifices were not made up for by the new life*, but the clause is infelicitous in its grammar and so the teacher does not recognize the position being presented. This clause could have been placed at the end of the paragraph to provide a macro-theme for the essay. The student has few resources for presenting evaluation, as evidenced by the way the student uses *were not made up for* to show evaluation in this clause. The reader is left wondering what this means, as Peter suggested.

Evaluation is also found in clauses 6 and 7, *the work was hard and paid little*. These clauses are an attempt to discuss the working conditions of immigrants, presenting the reality that immigrants found once in the U.S. Here, we see two evaluative meanings in *hard* and *little* that present the negative assessment identified by the writer. Unlike Texts Five and Six, we see very few qualities being presented in Text Seven. Unlike Text Five, which fully describes the working and living conditions of immigrants, and Text Six, which describes the working conditions of immigrants by focusing on the factories and their surroundings, this text does not fully describe the working and living conditions of immigrants. Clause 8 presents in rheme position another difficulty that immigrants faced, *constantly made aware of their differences*. Clause 9 presents another situation that was difficult for immigrants, *and by most nativists were seen as inferior and lower than the lowest class*. Here again we see a difficulty that immigrants faced, but this is again not linked to other difficulties. For instance, we see many claims that need to be further elaborated. The writer does not use an organizing device to introduce the difficulties or sacrifices made.

Unlike Texts Five and Six, in which elaboration is an important textual move, elaboration appears only in a few places in Text Seven. Clause 13 goes back to the idea of working conditions being *dangerous* and *hazardous,* elaborating on the word *hard* presented in clause 6. Clause 12 seems to support the idea that few made it and repeats the words *lowest class* to reiterate that immigrants were seen as *inferior.* Part of the rheme of clause 12, *were forced to things that most Americans wouldn't take as work,* also goes back to the idea of work presented in clause 6. It seems that this student is aware of repetition as a linguistic process to elaborate on the ideas. He would also benefit from attention to other ways that we saw enable the exemplification and clarification used in the more successful essays. As Peter puts it, in this text, "There's no real analysis. There's a list of some things that happened to people." This idea of a "list" is evidenced by the new information presented in the rheme but never developed or exemplified. The rheme to theme movement does not help the writer move from clause to clause in such a way that the points are built up in each clause. According to Peter, the student "talks about being seen as inferior—again, give some examples, maybe how were they seen as inferior, so analyze it." This means that the student needs to use elaboration. Each one of the clauses from this essay could be developed and expanded. Looking at the rhemes of each clause, we can see the potential of this essay if the ideas were expressed more fully and in greater detail.

The essay lacks the elaboration and language complexity that was present in Texts Five and Six. Peter finds that "there's no conclusion and they throw out some things, some sacrifices made." This "throwing out" is evidenced by the lack of organizational features that would enable this writer to make more links between the ideas presented, as in Text Five. Unlike Text Five, this text is not structured in such a way that would enable the presentation of historical information about the working and living conditions of immigrants. The essay also does not take a position that addresses the question directly and never mentions whether or not the trip was worth the new life. The text seems to argue the position that that the trip was not worth the new life, but this is never stated or supported effectively. This exemplifies the lack of effective resources found in essays that were considered unsuccessful in adequately addressing the prompt. The main feature that was not present was elaboration. Unsuccessful essays, like Text Seven, did not develop the ideas that were presented by providing details, examples, or further clarification. These essays were not organized in a way that showed the points to be developed, nor did they acknowledge opposing viewpoints through the use of projection, modality, and concession.

## Discussion

While we cannot generalize to all expository writing in school history, we can point out some important features that were present in the 11th-grade sample. As Figure 5.4 demonstrates, the movement toward the highly valued in exposition goes from the resources that were used in the 8th-grade corpus to the resources presented in the 11th-grade corpus.

| | |
|---|---|
| **Theme** | No clear pattern of theme<br>Interpersonal themes that construct a subjective and hortatory style<br>Macro-theme that does not present or partially presents the writer's position on the question |
| **Logical Connections** | Conjunctions of *addition* that organize the text<br>Consequential conjunction *because* to show *cause*<br>Pervasive interactional style features |
| **Elaboration** | through repetition<br>Restating macro-theme |

| | |
|---|---|
| **Theme** | Use of theme as organizing device<br>*Constant theme* and *rheme to theme* movement<br>Macro-theme that presents the writer's position on the question by answering it |
| **Logical Connections** | Conjunctions of *cause* and *condition*<br>Grammatical metaphor: Cause marked through verbs<br>More academic style, fewer interactional discourse features |
| **Elaboration** | through repetition, synonymy, and grammatical metaphor<br>Restating macro-theme<br>Moving from general to specific by giving examples<br>Renaming and restating points |

| | |
|---|---|
| **Theme** | Use of theme as organizing device<br>Constant theme and rheme to theme movement<br>Marked themes that help structure essay<br>Rheme accumulates information that supports the development of the essay<br>Macro-theme that presents the writer's position on the question by answering it and provides a framework for the essay<br>Hyper-themes that provide a framework for each paragraph |
| **Logical Connections** | Conjunctions of *cause, condition,* and *concession*<br>Grammatical metaphor: Cause marked through verbs<br>More academic style, fewer interactional discourse features<br>Concession for acknowledging opposing viewpoints |
| **Elaboration** | through repetition, synonymy, grammatical metaphor, meronymy, and collocation<br>Restating macro-theme and hyper-themes<br>Moving from general to specific by giving examples<br>Renaming and restating points<br>Adding more detail or further specifying |

**Figure 5.4** Movement toward the highly valued in exposition in 8th and 11th grades.

*(continued)*

| **Evaluation** | *Resources for Appreciation*<br>Attributive processes that construct descriptions<br>Negative and positive assessments |
|---|---|
| | *Resources for Engagement*<br>**Projection** through mental processes to bring others' words into the text via direct quotation or indirect reference<br>**Concession** through conjunctions (e.g., *but, even though, although*) to acknowledge different points of view<br>**Modality** that expresses necessity and obligation (*have/had to*) to reiterate the inevitability of the situation for immigrants and to acknowledge alternative voices around a proposition or claim |
| | *Resources for Graduation*<br>Grading up and down through adverbs and other resources for intensifying evaluation |

**Figure 5.4 (continued)** Movement toward the highly valued in exposition in 8th and 11th grades.

Figure 5.4 shows the movement toward the highly valued in exposition in school history. Here, I highlight the additional resources used at the 11th-grade level. The thematic choices show effective organizing strategies for moving the essays forward, while the rheme is functional for the accumulation of information that supports the development of the essay. A macro-theme is used to present the writer's position on the topic and to give a purpose for the essay. Hyper-themes are used at the beginning of a paragraph and reiterated at the end, and they often follow a concessive pattern that enables writers to recognize an opposing viewpoint while at the same time presenting their own.

Elaboration is accomplished through more complex linguistic processes. These processes include meronymy, collocation, and grammatical metaphor. Elaboration enables the presentation of examples, clarifications, additional details, and explanations. Restating the macro-theme and hyper-themes is particularly relevant at the 11th-grade level.

Resources for evaluation appear at the 11th-grade level as important ways of presenting descriptions and judgments. The Appreciation resources enable the presentation of negative and positive evaluation, which helps writers build texts that acknowledge the difficulties of immigrants' conditions. Attributive processes are used to construe negative and positive assessments. In addition to the pattern in the use of Appreciation resources, Engagement, concerned with the source of attitudes, is used to include additional voices in the discourse through projection, modality, and concession. Projection through mental processes is used to acknowledge alternative sources, bringing others' words into the text and presenting different perspectives on the issues. Concession is used to acknowledge opposing points of view and present the writer's position. Modality indicating necessity and obligation is used to reiterate the inevitability of the situation for immigrants. The combination of these resources enables students to effectively accomplish the writing task.

In this chapter, we saw how certain linguistic features, such as elaboration, evaluation, and theme, are functional for writing the 11th-grade expository genre. The linguistic analysis presented has demonstrated that learning to structure texts in specific ways is crucial to students' success in school history writing. Writing an effective expository essay depends on using particular lexical and grammatical features that enable the presentation of a well-constructed essay, showing that being successful in school history writing depends on more than just having the content knowledge. Being successful depends on having the linguistic resources to demonstrate the content knowledge through language.

## Notes

1. The Appraisal framework uses capital letters for these constructs.
2. Students could take the position that it was *not* worth for immigrants to move to the U.S. However, the 11th-grade teachers' expectations were that students would say that even though immigrants had many difficulties, it was still worth it for them to move to the U.S.
3. Quotes from the essays within quotes from teachers are in italics.

# 6

## *Conclusions and Implications*

How is writing used and taught in 8th- and 11th-grade history classes in two school districts in California? What are the expectations for students' writing in history? What are the language features that enable students to write an exposition at the 8th- and 11th-grade levels in school history? What skills do 8th- and 11th-grade students need to reach the level they are expected? These research questions were addressed throughout this book. In this concluding chapter, I discuss what makes certain history writing expectations particular to this content area. In addition, I demonstrate how a focus on the language of history can be incorporated into teacher education and professional development programs in which teachers can develop their understanding of the nature of writing in history.

## Teaching Writing in History

In Chapter Three, we saw that teacher responses overwhelmingly emphasized the importance of writing in history. However, a discrepancy appeared when we considered teachers' perspectives on the role of writing in history and their emphasis on writing instruction. While teachers see writing as an important aspect of history, a number of other factors influence teachers' decisions about what to teach in history. The challenges that focus teachers discussed clearly affect their writing instruction in history. In reporting

*Knowing and Writing School History*, pages 125–136
Copyright © 2011 by Information Age Publishing
All rights of reproduction in any form reserved.

on their teaching of writing, most history teachers focused on aspects of organization and structure but did not recognize how linguistic features contribute to the organization and structure of writing. This is not surprising, given the fact that history teachers do not typically receive any kind of professional development in explicit ways to deal with language in their subject area. The findings presented in Chapter Three indicate that it would be beneficial for teachers to develop a better understanding of the role of language in history learning. They also point to the need for teacher education and professional development programs to assist teachers with ways to better incorporate writing instruction in history, which I address in this concluding chapter. Teachers can develop their knowledge of the significance of writing in history classes.

Chapters Four and Five showed how linguistic features realize the organization, structure, and development of essays. The text analyses presented in these chapters represent the larger corpus of 8th- and 11th-grade writing, and the examples presented in those chapters are representative of the variety and range of resources used by students at each grade level. Successful essays from both grade levels showed the power of elaboration in the construction of the expository genre. The analysis also showed that teachers have expectations in terms of how the historical information is to be presented and developed. Teachers' expectations are realized *in* and *through* the language used by students to demonstrate their historical understanding. Without an emphasis on the actual features of students' writing, advice on how to help students develop their language skills and increase their achievement in history can only be given based on assumptions about what constitutes "good writing," assumptions that often call on notions such as "clarity" and "development" without good understanding by teachers of how these abstract notions are realized in language. Teachers can gain knowledge of how specific lexical and grammatical choices in the presentation of historical information constitute effective and successful texts. Giving students opportunities to talk about text means apprenticing them into the discipline of history. Helping students to think like historians is a major goal in history education and can only be accomplished if students are able to read and write in school history.

The differing language patterns that students drew on to respond to the 11th-grade writing prompt show that even though both the 8th- and 11th-grade writing prompts elicited patterns of exposition, the kind of writing tasks were different. The 11th-grade task was more complex than the 8th-grade task, entailing the use of more complex grammatical and lexical resources, as was evidenced in Chapter Five. Therefore, this demonstrates that teachers must be aware of the language demands placed on students by different writing tasks, even when they elicit an exposition. Teachers should also consider the discipline-specific nature of history, which I attend to in the next section, as I present a summary of the results of the linguistic analyses.

## The Discipline-Specific Nature of School History Writing

This book demonstrated that history uses academic language in specific ways and points to the need to develop more effective means for assisting novice school history writers to manage the evaluative demands of writing an expository genre. History has its own expectations and typical discipline-specific linguistic choices that present and re-present historical interpretations and perspectives. Students must be able to organize the historical information they present. As we saw in Chapter Four, through the thematic choices, the writers signaled the organizational structure and created a highly structured text organized around what they were presenting. Cohesive resources such as pronouns were used to make links and establish relationships between elements of discourse. The expository writing tasks analyzed in this book showed that students must be able to present evaluative meanings when they write about history. Evaluative meanings are important in history because they enable the presentation of a position that the history student has taken. Functional linguistic research shows that evaluation is very important in history (Coffin, 2002; Martin, 2002; Oteiza, 2003). Resources for evaluation included Appreciation resources that writers used to present negative and positive assessments; Engagement resources of modality, projection, and concession used to bring in multiple voices as sources of evaluations; and Graduation resources used to scale up or down in value. The expression of concession is particularly relevant, as shown in the 11th-grade analysis, for writing about history, as student historians are supposed to acknowledge alternative viewpoints while presenting their own. Students are expected to approach the study of history as historians do and read and examine primary source documents, where students can explore different perspectives on historical events (California Department of Education, 2000, Introduction). Part of "thinking like a historian" (Greene, 1994) is drawing inferences based on historical evidence and considering historical documents as a corpus of evidence, not as isolated units (Wineburg, 1994). This requires that students consider multiple perspectives on historical events and that they represent those perspectives when they write. Therefore, to think and write like historians, students must assess the information and provide their own perspectives, while at the same time presenting and acknowledging the multiple angles that could be taken on an issue. This is at the heart of writing about history. To present these multiple perspectives, student historians rely on concession and contrast to acknowledge alternative viewpoints that could be taken on the issue.

History is highly dependent on the presentation of historical evidence. This means that to do history, historians must not only present an interpretation but also display how they reached that particular interpretation by providing historical evidence. Like historians, in responding to an expository writing task, history students must present a position and support it. The historical evidence that students use comes in the form of examples, clarifications, additional details, and restatements of ideas already presented. Students must use elaborating relationships to support their positions. It is not enough for student historians to present a specific interpretation or position; they must present how they reached that particular interpretation. This is accomplished through elaboration, as shown in Chapters Four and Five, which presented it as a key feature for students' presentation of their ideas and a distinguishing feature of the highly valued texts.

In addition, historians generally agree that expressing causal relations is a key component of knowing and writing history (Britt, Rout, Georgi, & Perfetti, 1994; Coffin, 2004; Halldén, 1997). To think critically about history, students need to be able to consider multiple causes for historical events, which is seen as an important aspect of history learning (California Department of Education, 2001). As Halldén (1997) points out, causal analysis is particularly important in historical writing, but students have difficulty expressing causality in writing. This suggests that developing control of causal relations is a critical component in students' apprenticeship into school history writing (Coffin, 2004, 2006). As shown in Chapter Four, expressing logical connections of cause and condition were part of the more highly valued essays at the 8th-grade level, emphasizing that expressing causality is indeed a critical component of school history writing.

## Accomplishing Goals, Overcoming Challenges: Supporting History Educators

Valuing history by emphasizing its significance since early on in schooling seems to be an important step in accomplishing the goals that history teachers hold and overcoming the current challenges they face. In most American schools, history is not introduced until the 5th grade. History and other areas of the social studies, as Burroughs, Groce, and Webeck (2005) found, are not taught enough in today's policy and high-stakes testing context. It is important to recognize the context in which history teachers are doing their work, where history is not emphasized and reading, math, and science are "the big things," as Peter stated.

This book highlighted that history teachers face several challenges in working in schools today, including the limited teaching of history, the pressure for coverage, and the lack of background knowledge of students. As presented in Chapter Three, these conditions all have an effect on the teaching of writing in history classes. Providing students with enough historical background to be able to develop their historical understanding is crucial, and this can only be achieved when history is considered an essential subject in school. As VanSledright (1997) argues, "[T]he more one knows the more one is in a position to learn, for the outcome of previous learning provides the context within which fresh learning may occur" (pp. 4–5). This shows the importance of historical content knowledge and background. Providing teaching conditions and school environments that support and sustain student learning is a key aspect of education (Darling-Hammond, 2004). It seems that an increase in students' background knowledge can only happen when the system recognizes the potential of history to improve students' learning in general.

As this book demonstrated, history learning is highly dependent on language, and more than any other subject, it holds the potential for improving students' writing skills. While teachers see writing as an important aspect of history, writing is mostly used as an assessment instrument rather than as a way to help students develop their understanding of history, or as "writing to learn." Writing to learn has been described by Writing across the Curriculum (WAC) proponents as writing that helps students discover new understandings by examining previous knowledge and realizing additional ideas (National Writing Project & Nagin, 2003). With the increasing number of diverse students, including mainstreamed ELLs, history teachers need to recognize the importance of an explicit attention to writing in helping students to advance their knowledge of history. History teachers need to be made aware of the role of language in students' demonstration of their historical understanding, and they need to receive professional development in explicit ways to deal with language in their subject area.

To participate in this kind of professional development with a focus on language, history teachers must be supported by school districts and continue to build on their expertise. Teachers need knowledge and skills in their subject matter, student learning methods, and varied teaching strategies to effectively develop procedures that will support student learning and help students achieve new standards. Districts need to develop a greater responsibility for supporting new and veteran teachers who will be able to provide the kind of expertise students need (Darling-Hammond, 2004). School districts have adopted novice models of teacher support and ongoing professional development that include mentoring, peer observation and coaching, study groups and subject matter-specific systems, ongoing seminars linked to practice, and school–university partnerships that involve collaborative research (Achinstein & Athanases, 2006; Darling-Hammond, 1998). Schools that enable teachers to plan together and offer them professional development time have shown increased success in addressing the needs of diverse learners (Darling-Hammond, 2004). These are elements that history teachers need in order to be successful and for the kind of work recommended here to be effective.

In addition to the support that history teachers need, more research on the application of the work presented here for work with teachers is needed. This book is positioned at the intersection between linguistics and education. The key challenge in any linguistics-based research in education is to find ways to bridge the complexity of linguistic descriptions and the applicability for educational purposes. Therefore, there is important work to be done in translating the complexity of the linguistic work presented in this book for use with teachers (e.g., Schleppegrell & de Oliveira, 2006; de Oliveira, 2010). More research in the area of applying the linguistic analyses presented is needed so that this work can more readily be applied in teacher education and professional development programs. In the next section, I outline some of the ways in which this book has pedagogical applications for the teaching of writing in school history. I explain how attention to specific language features can provide a framework for pedagogical considerations by providing examples from other essays from the corpus. In using the examples, I show how history teachers can use students' writing to raise their awareness of specific language features.

## Teaching Development and Analysis in School History: The Role of Theme, Evaluation, and Elaboration

As this book demonstrated, many students have not yet developed the grammatical and lexical features that enable the presentation of an organized and structured essay. Inexperienced writers draw on patterns of spoken language to organize their essays, described by focus teachers as "writing in a speaking style." These choices do not help the writers to construct a more distanced position, which is expected of history writing. These writers' language choices create a text that in history teachers' views is "subjective." As they develop, students move from more informal registers that draw on the language of interaction to more formal registers that use thematic progression to organize and present information. With the help of a teacher, the language resources needed to develop an effective exposition can be brought into focus. The less successful writers can notice that they have options for constructing a text that is more academic. They can learn that every meaning can be expressed in various ways. This knowledge can be attained by focusing on how different linguistic choices realize different social contexts. In this section, I present the value of theme and rheme in the organization and structuring of texts. In addition, I highlight ways that teachers can address evaluation and elaboration to assist students in developing their ideas.

History teachers need knowledge about how different lexical and grammatical choices construct the types of texts that are expected in academic contexts. An understanding of the functional meanings conveyed by these language choices can enable history teachers to effectively incorporate a focus on language in history classes. Writing an expository essay depends on more than just having the content knowledge; it depends on using particular lexical and grammatical features that enable the presentation of a well-constructed essay. The linguistic analyses presented have demonstrated that learning to structure texts in specific ways is crucial to students' success in school history writing.

The discussion of theme has shown that thematic choices are important for organizing and moving a text forward. Theme is functional for linking with prior discourse so that information can be accumulated. The macro-theme, or theme of the essay, is the most important thematic structure in school history. A macro-theme is known in school rhetoric as a *thesis statement*. It has a predictive function as to what will be developed in the essay. A hyper-theme is the theme of the paragraph, giving an orientation to what is to come and providing a framework for the paragraph. When hyper-themes are used effectively, they contribute to the overall organizational structure of the essay, helping the writer provide a framework for the ideas and helping the reader to follow what is being presented and developed. Looking at theme, hyper-theme, and macro-theme as points of departure for the clause, the paragraph, and the essay is a useful way to address text organization and structuring from a discourse semantic perspective. Teachers can examine how students are beginning their clauses and assist them in making choices that will provide effective organizing strategies for moving the essay forward.

Clause rhemes, and how they enable the presentation of evaluation and elaboration, can also be a focus of attention, especially in how they are functional for the accumulation of information that supports the development of the essay. Students can learn how to move from rheme to theme effectively through the use of condensation strategies such as demonstratives, pronominal reference, and other linguistic strategies that functional linguists have identified as useful rheme to theme resources, such as nominalization, which displays information that has been presented in verbs and whole clauses as nouns, a more sophisticated use of the rheme to theme development (Schleppegrell, 2004).

One of the major concerns that history teachers have with students' writing is their lack of development of their ideas in writing. The resources of evaluation and elaboration are ways of accomplishing the development that history teachers often find missing in students' essays. Rather than just asking students to "develop their ideas," it is suggested here that teachers can help students see how this development of ideas can be accomplished linguistically through the grammatical and lexical processes used to construe evaluation and elaboration.

Pedagogic intervention is a key aspect of moving students from where they are to where they are expected to be. Specifically, students can learn to use the linguistic resources that enable opposing viewpoints to be presented so that they are able to incorporate the multiple voices of history into their writing. This in turn would help them realize that history involves debates and opposing viewpoints. Part of "thinking like a historian," a goal of history teaching identified in the study, is being able to incorporate diverse points of view into one's writing. History is about interpretation, so historians are always representing it through a certain point of view. Therefore, the Engagement resources of projection, modality, and concession and what they enable writers to do should be a focus of pedagogy. History teachers can show effective ways for bringing in outside voices as support for students' positions by demonstrating how writers accomplish this. For instance, in another essay written at the 11th-grade level, the writer presented *Americans thought that immigrants were taking their jobs.* Teachers can point out how the mental process *thought* was used to introduce an idea, presenting an outside voice as supporting information. Teachers can point to several of these mental processes in students' texts and raise students' attention to these when they are reading history textbooks, since many textbooks use these types of verbs when they present debates or diverse points of view. This is an area where reading and writing connections are possible. In reading textbooks, students can be made aware of these types of verbs when they read about historical debates and diverse points of view and see how these verbs are being used in their textbooks to realize the nuances in meanings, noticing how their meanings differ or are similar. They can then practice how to introduce multiple perspectives into their writing by using some of the same verbs. Teachers can work on the reporting verbs that introduce thoughts and ideas and highlight the different meanings of these verbs. For instance, teachers can draw attention to differences between *claim, argue,* and *state,* pointing out that different verbs can be used to introduce an author's claims. These are a few suggestions that could be taken by professional development providers to develop workshops that would focus on certain linguistic features that would help teachers focus on the presentation of multiple perspectives, since this is an important feature of history writing. Again, the focus should be on the expression of historical points, so the function of linguistic features as tools for enabling the history student to accomplish subject-specific goals should be foregrounded.

In addition to the presentation of different positions, writers need to be able to evaluate how significant an event is, the consequences of past events, and major debates among historians concerning alternative interpretations of the past (California Department of Education, 2000). This evaluation requires the use of Appreciation resources such as the ones present in the 11th-grade writing sample. This book points to the need to develop more effective means for assisting novice school history writers to manage the evaluative demands of writing an expository genre. This can be accomplished through a discussion of the function of attributive processes in the presentation of evaluation. For example, in *The living conditions are better here as well,* the student uses the attributive process *are* to construct a comparison with *better.* The teacher can help students recognize when and where attributive processes are used and work with them to add qualities— or, in this case, a comparison—in order to describe. Teachers can also help students expand their lexical choices by focusing on several qualities that would provide descriptions. For example, in the case of the 11th-grade writing task, teachers can assist students in considering different qualities to describe the living and working conditions of immigrants. This approach can be an interactive co-construction of meaning, with the teacher and students considering different options from the system of evaluation that students can use as they describe.

A focus on evaluation can also be done as a way of connecting what students read to what they write. In reading textbooks or other sources, teachers can point out how evaluation is being accomplished through different language resources, such as adjectives. This should be done in the context of a reading passage in which students can examine how different qualities are presented by the writer. This is just one way that teachers could focus on evaluation resources. As this book showed, this area of meaning is especially important in school history writing, and more research in this area would yield other ways of focusing on evaluation in both reading and writing.

Elaboration helps writers develop their ideas throughout the essay. Writers need language resources to elaborate effectively. They need to know how to provide examples, clarify points, and provide additional details. Different grammatical processes that students use to elaborate show sophistication and language complexity. Teachers can focus on the process of elaboration by helping students restate something already presented, include additional details, clarify points already discussed, explain, exemplify, and further describe. Teachers can understand the processes through which development is accomplished, such as repetition, synonymy, meronymy, repetition, and grammatical metaphor. It is not suggested here that teachers use this terminology in the classroom or that they go in depth into the linguistic descriptions of these processes. The proposed approach is a focus on how these processes accomplish the history goals. What is important for an application of the work presented here is an emphasis on how these processes help writers show their historical knowledge through language. The key to any focus on language in history is to find the linguistic constructs that teachers can most readily adopt in their own teaching and determine the ways of talking about language that teachers find most accessible. This is instrumental in any kind of professional development and teacher education program grounded in a linguistic framework. A linguistic approach such as the one suggested here shows that learning how to manipulate the language in new ways can be very effective for students in developing their ideas.

Teachers can show students the potential of language to expand and elaborate their ideas. For example, clause rhemes are a good place to pay attention to, since rhemes are functional for the accumulation of information. If teachers have students break down their texts into themes and rhemes, they can alert students to places where they need to clarify, exemplify, include additional details, and reiterate main points, including the macro- and hyper-themes. Then, once students know how a theme/rheme categorization works, they can focus on developing their ideas themselves by analyzing clause rhemes to find how they elaborated their ideas and identify places they need to work on. Looking at a text clause by clause can help teachers see how language is construing the meanings students are trying to express. Although an intensive focus is time consuming, this type of language work, done on a regular basis, can enable teachers and students to talk about texts in very concrete ways.

## Providing Meaning-Based Feedback

Teachers need to focus on the meanings that student writers are attempting to express and help them develop a repertoire of language resources for writing the genres that are highly valued in history classrooms. Providing meaning-based feedback on students' writing is a useful way of focusing on the meanings that students are attempting to express. This type of feedback is especially important for ELLs. Rather than focusing on ELLs' language errors, a meaning-based approach would concentrate on the meanings that ELLs are constructing in the texts they write. Students should not be penalized for the language errors they make; instead, these "errors" should be seen as part of students' learning process as they develop new ways of making meaning in school history. To underline language as a meaning-making resource, teachers can provide feedback that goes beyond an identification of language errors to a productive meaning-based approach that focuses on different ways of presenting the same meanings.

## The Language of History: Developing Students' Literacy and Historical Understanding

Learning history means learning the language of history and how to express historical knowledge through language. History holds the potential to improve students' literacy while developing their historical understanding, since reading and writing are an integral part of history teaching and learning. As one teacher put it, "Writing and history are perfectly suited to one another; writing helps students understand the history; history is a great subject for practicing a huge variety of writing skills" (Jo, 5th-grade teacher). History can provide a motivating environment in which students can develop as readers and writers. This content area can serve as a medium to improving students' reading and writing in general because students can develop knowledge about disciplinary expectations—how writing for history may be different from writing in other school subjects. The insights gained from the history teachers in this book can help teacher educators recognize the range of ways that writing is addressed in school history. They can also help professional development providers to plan for workshops and presentations that focus on writing development across grade levels.

In order to improve students' literacy in history, we first need to prepare history teachers to provide the kind of instruction that will address the language of history. History teachers would benefit from a better understanding of the role of language in students' demonstration of their historical understanding. This is not to ask teachers to completely change what they have been doing in their classes, but it is to ask them to (re)consider the way they focus on language in history classrooms. This means that teacher educators and professional development providers need to take an active role in raising teachers' awareness of the role and power of language in reading and writing about history.

The work described in this chapter requires the development of systematic and clear methods and approaches to making a linguistic focus accessible and usable for practicing history teachers. There is still a lot to be done in this area. Research is needed on how teachers develop an understanding of the role of language in history and how they can best approach language in their subject area.

In order to accomplish the goal of higher student achievement in history, we need to understand the language resources students need to control to be successful. This book has provided a more complete picture of the linguistic knowledge and skills history students need in order to be successful in school history writing. The book identified a number of grammatical and lexical resources that students draw on when writing an expository essay in school history. When these resources are considered together, we can begin to see the complex nature of the expository writing task in school history. Knowing and writing history depend on opportunities for students to manipulate texts so that they can develop new ways of making meaning that correspond to teachers' expectations for expository writing. If students are to be critical thinkers, readers, and writers of school history, they need an explicit focus on language and how it constructs the perspectives and interpretations pervasive in history discourse. Without such a focus, students will continue to consider history just a "memorization of facts," and not a place where interpretation is at the heart of learning to think like a historian.

APPENDIX A

# *Questionnaire*

**Q 1** Think about two very different classes you teach, and please tell us a little about your students in terms of their academic preparedness, language backgrounds, and performance in writing.

Indicate the period, class title, and groups of students served (i.e., ELLs, Honors) for Class 1: _____

_____

Class 1: academic preparedness, language backgrounds, performance in writing _____

_____

Indicate the period, class title, and groups of students served (i.e., ELLs, Honors) for Class 2. _____

_____

Class 2: academic preparedness, language backgrounds, performance in writing _____

_____

**Q 2** As you know, there are many instruments teachers use to evaluate their students. Think about all the different ways you evaluate your students in history. From the following list, please check off which of these evaluation tools you use for Class 1.

☐ multiple choice questions, true/false, or matching
☐ short answer responses
☐ individual oral presentations
☐ informational group presentations to the class
☐ reader's theater or dramatic enactments
☐ outlining book chapter
☐ research paper
☐ argument writing
☐ visual representation of historical concepts
☐ longer (2–5 page) essays
☐ special projects (please specify) _____
☐ Other (please specify) _____

From the following list, please check off which of these evaluation tools you use for Class 2.

☐ multiple choice questions, true/false, or matching
☐ short answer responses
☐ individual oral presentations
☐ informational group presentations to the class
☐ reader's theater or dramatic enactments
☐ outlining book chapter
☐ research paper
☐ argument writing
☐ visual representation of historical concepts
☐ longer (2–5 page) essays
☐ special projects (please specify) _____
☐ Other (please specify) _____

**Q 3** What role do the History–Social Science standards play in your teaching, if any?

**Q 4** What role do you think writing has in a history class, if any?

**Q** **5** Sometimes history teachers provide writing instruction. Has any of your history teaching been something you might call "teaching writing"? Please explain.

**Q** **6** If you assign writing in your classes, what kinds of writing do you typically assign? Why?

**Q** **7** Are there any recurring problems you have noticed in your students' writing? If so, please list them below and put an asterisk next to the most prominent problem.

Recurring problem 1: _____

Recurring problem 2: _____

Recurring problem 3: _____

Other recurring problems: _____

Why do you think these problems are frequent in your students' writing?

**Q** **8** How many years have you been teaching?

**Q** **9** What grades have you taught? Please check below:

☐ ☐ ☐ ☐ ☐ ☐ ☐ ☐ ☐ ☐ ☐ ☐ ☐
K   1st   2nd   3rd   4th   5th   6th   7th   8th   9th   10th   11th   12th

**Q** **10** Please indicate your Degree(s), Subject(s), and Institution(s).

Q **11**  Please indicate your Teaching Credential(s), Subject(s), and Institution(s).

Q **12**  Please indicate in which district you currently teach.

Q **13**  Please add any other comments.

# *Interview 1 Questions*

Interviewer: Luciana de Oliveira

Date/Time/Location: _____

Interviewee: _____

Grades taught: _____

I'd like to thank you again for completing the questionnaire and for agreeing to meet with me today. I really appreciate your taking time to answer these interview questions. As you know, I'm interested in teacher practice in history classes and the challenges students face in history. So, the questions I'm going to ask you today are related to those topics. I'm going to ask you to be really honest in your answers. I'm not here to evaluate you or your teaching; I'm here to learn as much as I can from you.

1. What is the most rewarding aspect for you in being a history teacher?
2. What is the most challenging aspect for you in being a history teacher?
3. Could you tell me about the kinds of evaluation you use in your classes?

4. Could you tell me a little bit about your experience teaching English learners in your classes?

5. Many history teachers say that students have a lot of problems when they write, what do you think is the central problem (or problems) in student writing?

6. What kinds of writing assignments do you give students? Could you describe them?

7. In your questionnaire, you mentioned . . . . . . can you tell me a little more about . . . .

8. In your questionnaire, you mentioned . . . . . . can you tell me a little more about . . . .

9. Is there anything else you would like to add?

APPENDIX **C**

## *Interview 2 Questions*

Interviewee: _____

Date/Time/Location: _____

Grades taught: _____

1.  I'd like to take a look at the prompt before we start talking about the essays.
    **Could you please read the whole prompt?**

2.  When you look at the question that students were supposed to address, . . . **What would the best answer to this question be? In other words, what would you expect students to include in their answer?**

3.  After that, students were asked to . . . **Based on the kinds of things you addressed in class with them, what would you expect their answer to cover?**

4.  Under "task" students were asked to "provide a clear thesis." **What might that look like to you?**

5.  Students were also asked to "provide evidence." **What would you expect students to include here?**

6. Students were also asked to "analyze how that evidence supports your thesis." **For this topic, what do you think students should include?**

7. Students are often asked to construct a well-organized essay. **What do you think the elements are for such "well-organized essay? In other words, what would constitute "good organization" for you based on your experience?**

8. Now let's look at the essays you selected as strong, weak, and middle. **Can you show me the strong ones? Why did you select this one? Why do you think it is strong? Can you point to specific aspects of the essay that make it strong? Why is that?**
   What demonstrates students know (or don't know) the topic/subject here in this essay?

9. Now let's look at the essays that you consider weak or needing more work.
   **Why did you select this one? Why do you think it needs more work? Can you point to specific aspects of the essay that make it weak? Why is that?**
   What demonstrates students know (or don't know) the topic/subject here in this essay?

10. Now let's look at the essay that you consider middle.
    **Why did you select this one? Why do you think it sort of in the middle? Can you point to specific aspects of the essay? Why is that?**
    What demonstrates students know (or don't know) the topic/subject here in this essay?

11. Based on the things we talked about today, what do you think can be done for students and their writing skills in history?

12. When you think about what professional development services could provide you, what comes to your mind when you look at these essays now that you have some ideas about their strengths and things students need to improve? Kind of a wish list for professional development providers.

# References

Achinstein, B., & Athanases, S. Z. (Eds.). (2006). *Mentors in the making: Developing new leaders for new teachers.* New York: Teachers College Press.

Achugar, M., & M. J. Schleppegrell (2005). Beyond connectors: The construction of cause in history textbooks. *Linguistics and Education, 16*(3), 298–318.

Bailey, A. L., & Butler, F. A. (2002). *An evidentiary framework for operationalizing academic language for broad application to K–12 education: A design document.* University of California, Los Angeles: National Center for Research on Evaluation, Standards, and Student Testing (CRESST).

Ball, C. C., Dice, L., & Bartholomae, D. (1990). Telling secrets: Student readers and disciplinary authorities. In R. Beach & S. Hynds (Eds.), *Developing discourse practices in adolescence and adulthood* (pp. 337–358). Norwood, NJ: Ablex.

Bakhtin, M. M. (1981). *The dialogic imagination.* (C. Emerson & M. Holquist, Trans.). Austin, TX: University of Texas Press.

Beck, I. L., & McKeown, M. G. (1994). Outcomes of history instruction: Paste-up accounts. In M. Carretero & J. F. Voss (Eds.), *Cognitive and instructional processes in history and the social sciences* (pp. 237–256). Hillsdale, NJ: Erlbaum Associates.

Beck, I. L., McKeown, M. G., & Gromoll, E. W. (1989). Learning from social studies texts. *Cognition and Instruction, 6*(2), 99–158.

Beck, I. L., McKeown, M. G., Sinatra, G. M., & Loxterman, J. A. (1991). Revising social studies text from a text-processing perspective: Evidence of improved comprehensibility. *Reading Research Quarterly, 26,* 251–276.

Britt, M. A., Rout, J., Georgi, M. C., & Perfetti, C. A. (1994). Learning from history texts: From causal analysis to argument models. In G. Leinhardt, I.

L. Beck, & C. Stainton (Eds.), *Teaching and learning in history* (pp. 47–84). Hillsdale, NJ: Erlbaum.

Brophy, J. J. (1992). Fifth-grade U.S. History: How one teacher arranged to focus on key ideas in depth. *Theory and Research in Social Education, 20*(2), 141–155.

Burroughs, S., Groce, E., & Webeck, M. L. (2005). Social studies education in the age of testing and accountability. *Educational Measurement: Issues and Practice, 24*(3), 13–20.

California Department of Education. (2000). *History–Social Science content standards for California public schools* [Electronic version]. Retrieved May 20, 2005 from http://www.cde.ca.gov/be/st/ss/hstmain.asp

California Department of Education. (2001). *History–Social Science framework for California public schools.* Retrieved from http://www.projectsea.org/history _social_science.pdf

California Department of Education. (2010). Statewide number of English learners. Retrieved from http://dq.cde.ca.gov/dataquest

Carretero, M., & Voss, J. F. (Eds.). (1994). *Cognitive and instructional processes in history and the social sciences.* Hillsdale: Erlbaum.

Chambliss, M. J. (1994). Why do readers fail to change their beliefs after reading persuasive text? In R. Garner & P. A. Alexander (Eds.), *Beliefs about text and about instruction with text* (pp. 75–92). Hillsdale, NJ: Erlbaum.

Christie, F. (2002). *Classroom discourse analysis: A functional perspective.* New York: Continuum.

Coffin, C. (1997). Constructing and giving value to the past: An investigation into secondary school history. In F. Christie & J. R. Martin (Eds.), *Genres and institutions: Social processes in the workplace and school* (pp. 196–230). London: Cassell.

Coffin, C. (2002). The voices of history: Theorizing the interpersonal semantics of historical discourses. *Text, 22*(4), 503–528.

Coffin, C. (2004). Learning to write history: The role of causality. *Written Communication, 21*(3), 261–289.

Coffin, C. (2006). *Historical discourse: The language of time, cause, and evaluation.* New York: Continuum.

Coffin, C., & Hewings, A. (2004). IELTS as preparation for tertiary writing: Distinctive interpersonal and textual strategies. In L. J. Ravelli & R. Ellis (Eds.), *Analysing academic writing: Contextualized frameworks* (pp. 153–171). New York: Continuum.

Colombi, M. C. (2002). Academic language development in Latino students' writing in Spanish. In M. J. Schleppegrell & M. C. Colombi (Eds.), *Developing advanced literacy in first and second languages: Meaning with power* (pp. 67–86). Mahwah, NJ: Erlbaum.

Darling-Hammond, L. (1998). Teacher learning that supports student learning. *Educational Leadership, 55*(5), 6–11.

Darling-Hammond, L. (2004). Inequality and the right to learn: Access to qualified teachers in California's public schools. *Teachers College Record, 106*(10), 1936–1966.

de Oliveira, L. C. (2008). "History doesn't count": Challenges of teaching history in California schools. *The History Teacher, 41*(3), 363–378.

de Oliveira, L. C. (2010). Nouns in history: Packaging information, expanding explanations, and structuring reasoning. *The History Teacher, 43*(2), 1–13.

Downey, M. T., & Fischer, F. (2000). Responding to the winds of change in history education. *The History Teacher, 34*(1), 21–28.

Downey, M. T., & Levstik, L. S. (1991). Teaching and learning history. In J. P. Shaver (Ed.), *Handbook of research on social studies teaching and learning* (pp. 400–410). New York: Macmillan.

Eggins, S., Wignell, P., & Martin, J. R. (1993). The discourse of history: distancing the recoverable past. In M. Guadessy (Ed.), *Register analysis: Theory and practice* (pp. 75–109). London: Pinter Publishing.

Eskey, D. (1993). Reading and writing as both cognitive process and social behavior. In J. G. Carson & I. Leki (Eds.), *Reading in the composition classroom: Second language perspectives* (pp. 221–233). Boston, MA: Heinle & Heinle.

Fillmore, L. W., & Snow, C. (2000). *What teachers need to know about language.* Special report for the Center for Applied Linguistics. Retrieved from ERIC database. (ED444379).

Ferris, D., & Roberts, B. (2001). Error feedback in L2 writing classes: How explicit does it need to be? *Journal of Second Language Writing, 10*(3), 161–184

Fries, P. (1983). On the status of Theme in English: Arguments from discourse. In S. Petofi & E. Sozer (Eds.), *Micro and macro connexity of texts* (pp. 116–152). Hamburg: Helmut Buske.

Fries, P. (1995). Themes, methods of development, and texts. In R. Hasan & P. H. Fries (Eds.), *On subject and theme: from the perspective of functions in discourse* (pp. 317–360). Philadelphia, PA: John Benjamins.

Gee, J. P. (2002). Literacies, identities, and discourses. In M. J. Schleppegrell & M. C. Colombi (Eds.), *Developing advanced literacy in first and second languages: Meaning with power* (pp. 159–175). Mahwah, NJ: Erlbaum.

Greene, S. (1994). The problems of learning to think like a historian: Writing history in the culture of the classroom. *Educational Psychologist 29*(2), 89–96.

Halldén, O. (1986). Learning history. *Oxford Review of Education, 12*(1), 53–66.

Halldén, O. (1997). Conceptual change and the learning of history. *International Journal of Educational Research, 27*(3), 201–210.

Halldén, O. (1998). Personalization in historical descriptions and explanations. *Learning and Instruction, 8*(2), 131–139.

Halliday, M. A. K. (1993). Towards a language-based theory of learning. *Linguistics and Education, 5*(2), 93–116.

Halliday, M. A. K. (1994). *An introduction to functional grammar* (2nd ed.). London: Arnold.

Halliday, M. A. K., & Hasan, R. (1976). *Cohesion in English.* London: Longman.

Halliday, M. A. K., & Hasan, R. (1989). *Language, context, and text: Aspects of language in a social-semiotic perspective.* Oxford: Oxford University Press.

Halliday, M. A. K., & Martin, J. R. (Eds.). (1993). *Writing science: Literacy and discursive power.* Pittsburgh, PA: University of Pittsburgh Press.

Halliday, M. A. K., & Matthiessen, C. M. (2004). *An introduction to functional grammar.* London: Arnold.

Harniss, M. K., Dickson, S. V., Kinder, D., & Hollenbeck, K. L. (2001). Textual problems and instructional solutions: Strategies for enhancing learning from published history textbooks. *Reading & Writing Quarterly, 17*(2), 127–150.

Hennings, D. G. (1993). On knowing and reading history. *Journal of Reading, 36*(5), 362–370.

Kachaturoff, G. (1982). Textbook and selection: A professional responsibility. *The Social Studies, 73*(1), 32–56.

Kinder, D., Bursuck, B., & Epstein, M. (1992). An evaluation of history textbooks. *Journal of Special Education, 25*(4), 472–491.

Kress, G. (1997). *Before writing: Rethinking the paths to literacy.* London: Routledge.

Langer, J. (1992). Speaking of knowing: Conceptions of understanding in academic disciplines. In A. Herrington, & C. Moran (Eds.), *Writing, teaching, and learning in the disciplines* (pp. 69–85). New York: The Modern Language Association of America.

Lapp, M. S., Grigg, W. S., & Tay Lim, B. S. (2002). *The Nation's report card: U.S. history 2001.* Washington, DC: National Center for Education Statistics, Office of Educational Research and Improvement, U.S. Department of Education.

Lave, J., & Wenger, E. (1991). *Situated learning: Legitimate peripheral participation.* Cambridge: Cambridge University Press.

Leinhardt, G. (2000). Lessons on teaching and learning in history from Paul's pen. In P. N. Stearns, P. Seixas, & S. Wineburg (Eds.), *Knowing, teaching, and learning history: National and international perspectives* (pp. 223–245). New York: New York University Press.

Leinhardt, G., Beck, I. L., & Stainton, C. (Eds.). (1994). *Teaching and learning in history.* Hillsdale, NJ: Erlbaum.

Leinhardt, G., Stainton, C., & Virji, S. M. (1994). A sense of history. *Educational Psychologist, 29*(2), 79–88.

Leinhardt, G., Stainton, C., Virji, S. M., & Odoroff, E. (1994). Learning to reason in history: Mindlessness to mindfulness. In M. Carretero & J. F. Voss (Eds.), *Cognitive and instructional processes in history and the social sciences* (pp. 131–158). Hove, U.K.: Erlbaum.

Leung, C. (2001). Evaluation of content-language learning in the mainstream classroom. In B. Mohan, C. Leung, & C. Davidson (Eds.), *English as a second language in the mainstream: Teaching, learning and identity* (pp. 177–198). Harlow, England: Longman.

Levstik, L. S., & Pappas, C. C. (1992). New directions for studying historical understanding. *Theory and Research in Social Education, 20*(4), 369–385.

Martin, J. R. (1983). Conjunction: The logic of English text. In J. S. Petofi & E. Sozer (Eds.), *Micro and macro connexity of texts* (pp. 1–72). Hamburg: Helmut Buske Verlag.

Martin, J. R. (1985). Process and text: two aspects of human semiosis. In J. D. Benson & W. S. Greaves (Eds.), *Systemic perspectives on discourse,* Vol. 1 (pp. 248–274. Norwood, NJ: Ablex.

Martin, J. R. (1989). *Factual writing: exploring and challenging reality.* Oxford: Oxford University Press.

Martin, J. R. (1992). *English text.* Amsterdam: John Benjamins.

Martin, J. R. (2002). Writing history: Construing time and value in discourses of the past. In M. J. Schleppegrell & M. C. Colombi (Eds.), *Developing advanced literacy in first and second languages: Meaning with power* (pp. 87–118) Mahwah, NJ: Erlbaum.

Martin, J. R. (2004). Mourning: How we get aligned. *Discourse & Society, 15*(2–3), 321–344.

Martin, J. R., & Rose, D. (2003). *Working with discourse: Meaning beyond the clause.* London: Continuum.

Martin, J. R., & Rothery, J. (1986). What a functional approach to the writing task can show teachers about "good writing." In B. Couture (Ed.), *Functional approaches to writing* (pp. 241–265). London: Frances Pinter.

Martin, J. R., & Wodak, R. (2003). Introduction. In J. R. Martin & R. Wodak (Eds.), *Re/reading the past: Critical and functional perspectives on time and value* (pp. 1–16). Philadelphia, PA: John Benjamins.

McCarthy Young, K., & Leinhardt, G. (1998). Writing from primary documents: A way of knowing in history. *Written Communication, 15*(1), 25–68.

McKeown, M. G., & Beck, I. L. (1994). Making sense of accounts of history: Why young students don't and how they might. In G. Leinhardt, I. L. Beck, & C. Stainton (Eds.), *Teaching and learning in history* (pp. 1–26). Hillsdale, NJ: Lawrence Erlbaum Associates.

Merriam, S. B. (1998). *Qualitative research and case study applications in education* (Revised and expanded ed.). San Francisco: Jossey-Bass Inc.

Merriam, S. B. (2002). *Qualitative research in practice: Examples for discussion and analysis.* San Francisco: Jossey-Bass Publishers.

Mitchell, S., & Andrews, R. (1994). Learning to operate successfully in advanced level history. In A. Freedman & P. Medway (Eds.), *Learning and teaching genre* (pp. 81–103). Portsmouth, NH: Heinemann.

Mohan, B.A. (1986). *Language and content.* Reading, MA: Addison-Wesley.

Monte-Sano, C. (2008). Qualities of effective writing instruction in history classrooms: A cross-case comparison of two teachers' practices. *American Educational Research Journal, 45*(4), 1045–1079.

National Assessment of Educational Progress. (2001), *NAEP 2001 U.S. History Report Card: Findings from the National Assessment of Educational Progress.* Princeton, NJ: Author.

National Council for the Social Studies. (2004). *Expectations of excellence: Curriculum standards for social studies.* Retrieved from http://www.socialstudies.org/standards/

National Writing Project, & Nagin, C. (2003). *Because writing matters: Improving student writing in our schools.* San Francisco, CA: Jossey-Bass.

Newmann, F. M. (1988). Can depth replace coverage in the high school curriculum? *Phi Delta Kappan, 69*(5), 345–348.

Newmann, F. M. (1991). Higher order thinking in the teaching of social studies: Connections between theory and practice. In J. F. Voss, D. N. Perkins, & J. W. Segal (Eds.), *Informal reasoning and education* (pp. 381–400). Hillsdale, NJ: Erlbaum.

Oteiza, T. (2003). How contemporary history is presented in Chilean middle school textbooks. *Discourse & Society, 14*(5), 639–660.

Paxton, R. J. (1999). A deafening silence: History textbooks and the students who read them. *Review of Educational Research, 69*(3), 315–339.

Perfetti, C., Britt, M. A., Rouet, J., Georgi, M , & Mason, R. A. (1994). How students use texts to learn and reason about historical uncertainty. In M. Carretero & J. F. Voss (Eds.), *Cognitive and instructional processes in history and the social sciences* (pp. 257–283). Hove, U.K.: Erlbaum.

Pretorius, E. J. (1996). A profile of causal development amongst ten-year-olds: Implications for reading and writing. *Reading and Writing, 8*(5), 385–406.

Ravitch, D. R., & Finn, C. E. (1987). *What do our 17-year-olds know? A report on the first national assessment of history and literature.* New York: Harper and Row.

Schaffer, J. (1995). *Teaching the multiparagraph essay: A sequential nine-week unit.* San Diego, CA: Jane Schaffer Publications.

Schleppegrell, M. (2001). Linguistic features of the language of schooling. *Linguistics and Education, 12*(4), 431–459.

Schleppegrell, M. J. (2004). *The language of schooling: A functional linguistics perspective.* Mahwah, NJ: Erlbaum.

Schleppegrell, M. J. (2005). Technical writing in a second language: The role of grammatical metaphor. In L. J. Ravelli & R. A. Ellis (Eds.), *Analysing academic writing: Contextualized frameworks* (pp. 172–189). New York: Continuum.

Schleppegrell, M. J. (2006). The linguistic features of advanced language use: the grammar of exposition. In H. Byrnes (Ed.), *Advanced language learning: The contribution of Halliday and Vygotsky* (pp. 134–146). London: Continuum.

Schleppegrell, M. J., Achugar, M., & Oteiza, T. (2004). The grammar of history: Enhancing content-based instruction through a functional focus on language. *TESOL Quarterly, 38*(1), 67–93.

Schleppegrell, M. J., & de Oliveira, L. C. (2006). An integrated language and content approach for history teachers. *Journal of English for Academic Purposes, 5*(4), 254–268.

Sizer, T. R. (2004). *Horace's compromise: The dilemma of the American high school* (4th ed.). Boston, MA: Mariner Books.

Spoehr, K. T., & Spoehr, L. W. (1994). Learning to think historically. *Educational Psychologist, 29*(2), 71–77.

Stearns, P. N., Seixas, P., & Wineburg, S. (Eds.). (2000). *Knowing, teaching, and learning history: National and international perspectives.* New York: New York University Press.

Stockton, S. (1995). Writing in history: Narrating the subject of time. *Written Communication, 12*(1), 47–73.

Stodolsky, S. S. (1988). *The subject matters.* Chicago: University of Chicago Press.

Strauss, A. L. (1987). *Qualitative analysis for social scientists.* New York: Cambridge University Press.

Stuckey, S., & Salvucci, L. (2003). *Call to freedom: Beginnings to 1914.* Austin: Harcourt Brace & Co.

Thornton, S. J. (1991). Teacher as curriculum-instructional gatekeeper in social studies. In J. P. Shaver (Ed.), *Handbook of research on social studies teaching and learning* (pp. 237–248). New York: Macmillan.

Tyson, H., & Woodward, A. (1989). Why students aren't learning very much from textbooks. *Educational Leadership, 47,* 14–17.

Unsworth, L. (1999). Developing critical understanding of the specialised language of school science and history texts: A functional grammatical perspective. *Journal of Adolescent & Adult Literacy, 42*(7), 508–521.

VanSledright, B. (1997). On the importance of historical positionality to thinking about and teaching history. *International Journal of Social Education, 12*(2), 1–18.

van Hover, S. D., & Yeager, E. (2004). Challenges facing beginning history teachers: An exploratory study. *International Journal of Social Education, 19*(1), 8–21.

Veel, R., & Coffin, C. (1996). Learning to think like an historian: The language of secondary school history. In R. Hasan & G. Williams (Eds.), *Literacy in Society* (pp. 191–231). London: Longman.

Voss, J. F., Carretero, M., Kennet, J., & Silfies, L. N. (1994). The collapse of the Soviet Union: A case study in causal reasoning. In M. Carretero & J. F. Voss (Eds.), Cognitive and instructional processes in history and the social sciences (pp. 403–429). Hillsdale, NJ: Erlbaum.

Voss, J. F., & Wiley, J. (2000). A case study of developing historical understanding via instruction: The importance of integrating text components and constructing arguments. In P. N. Stearns, P. Seixas, & S. Wineburg (Eds.), *Knowing, teaching, and learning history: National and international perspectives* (pp. 375–389). New York: New York University Press.

Wells, G. (2002). Learning and teaching for understanding: The key role of collaborative knowledge building. *Social Constructivist Teaching, 9,* 1–41.

Wineburg, S. S. (1991). On the reading of historical texts: Notes on the breach between school and academy. *American Educational Research Journal, 28*(3), 495–519.

Wineburg, S. S. (1994). The cognitive representation of historical texts. In G. Leinhardt, I. L. Beck, & C. Stainton (Eds.), *Teaching and learning in history* (pp. 85–135). Hillsdale, NJ: Erlbaum.

Wineburg, S. S. (2001). *Historical thinking and other unnatural acts: Charting the future of teaching the past.* Philadelphia: Temple University Press.

Wineburg, S. S., & Fournier, J. (1994). Contextualized thinking in history. In M. Carretero & J. F. Voss (Eds.), *Cognitive and instructional processes in history and the social sciences* (pp. 285–308). Hillsdale, NJ: Erlbaum.

Wineburg, S. S., & Wilson, S. M. (1991). Subject matter knowledge in the teaching of history. In J. Brophy (Ed.), *Advances in research on teaching: A research manual* (pp. 305–347). Greenwich, CT: JAI Press Inc.